CW00815961

RARE BIRDS
TRUE STYLE

RARE BIRDS
TRUE STYLE

EXTRAORDINARY INTERIORS,
PERSONAL COLLECTIONS & SIGNATURE LOOKS

VIOLET NAYLOR-LEYLAND

PRINCIPAL PHOTOGRAPHY BY ANDREW FARRAR

RIZZOLI
NEW YORK

New York Paris London Milan

CONTENTS

INTRODUCTION
VIOLET NAYLOR-LEYLAND

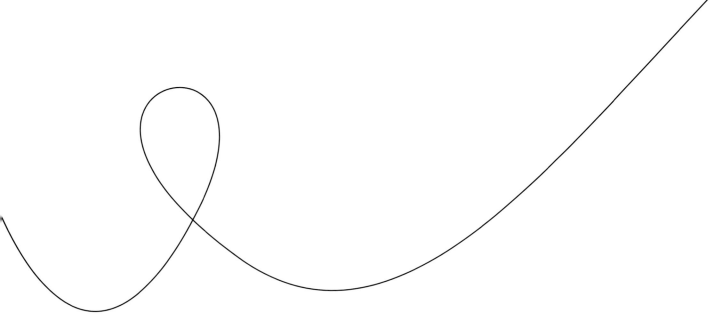

DRESSING WELL IS ONE THING, having style is another, but developing a signature taste that distinguishes you from all others is something more unusual and rather special. I have always been fascinated by other people's style. Whether it is considered good or bad has never mattered. What is interesting to me is the story it tells.

The light, colours, and textures of the world in which we grew up, reflected in our childhood homes, our parents' taste or the exterior landscape, have a strong impact. Whether we ride comfortably alongside that, as life meanders, take little snippets from it, or rebel directly, our environment from such a formative time, like it or not, is imprinted in our visual memory.

Interwoven along the three-year journey to make this book were wonderfully honest, original, funny, and moving tales told by the seventeen people included. In our final chapter, Sabine Getty speaks so beautifully about honouring her inner child with the creation of her fantastical Schiaparelli wedding dress. As I listened to all these stories, poignant memories of my own came flooding back, inadvertently prompting me to learn why I created a book about individual style in the first place.

My own parents—curious creatures of habit—sprung to mind. My father stuck to a strict dress code and my mother, who hated shopping, wore the same Indian mirrored skirt she had from when she was sixteen almost every day for twenty years until all the mirrors and embroidery rubbed off, exposing two holes where her bottom cheeks were. My father finally put his foot down, rang his friend the designer Rifat Ozbek to say his wife's wardrobe needed updating, and begged him to take her shopping. After a day in London, she returned home with a brand new, slightly darker red almost identical Indian mirrored skirt.

On the other hand, my parents regarded me as an anomaly for being drawn to clothing, and wanting to discover anything and everything there was to know about it.

As a small child, I remember spending hours in my mother's walk-in wardrobe, climbing up and down the pine shoe rack, trying on her wedding dress and hiding along the top shelf among her hat boxes until someone came to lift me down for tea. It was a happy spot. On my fifth birthday I was sent a red, white, and black spotted Cruella de Vil minidress by my actress godmother, Rachel Ward, in Australia. I wore it almost until it became a scarf. Uncannily, I often wear that exact colour trio still.

Aged six, I experienced my first yearning for a pale pink tulle ballet dress hung near the entrance of John Lewis in Peterborough. My mother really did not want to buy it for me. She preferred rustic Fair Isle jumpers, braces, corduroys, and smock dresses. Coming from the Northumberland countryside, surrounded by artistic bohemian siblings, perhaps this felt more natural to her. Certainly, pink nylon freaked her out. After months of my whining, she told my father to do the deed and buy it for me for Christmas. The thrill of this present was supreme. So, in it went to join Cruella de Vil in the nursery's fancy dress trunk, the lid of which was rarely shut. Now when my own children beg for a Minions hoodie, my heart sinks and I empathise fully.

ABOVE
A trio of brooches given to Violet by her grandmother Belinda Lambton.

Our book's opening chapter features the wonderful Victoria Grant, who tells the story of her grandfather buying her a pair of rainbow trousers she so badly wanted. She recognised this small but meaningful gesture as setting her creativity free.

When I was fifteen, my mother took me on a fleeting visit to Top Shop. We spotted the grooviest 1960s-style tan suede and sheepskin-trimmed coat like the one Kate Hudson wears in the film *Almost Famous* (2000), but this was floor-length. I had written it off in my mind, deciding I did not deserve to look that cool, perhaps because, for some time, I had been bullied at school for "having long hair" and being "weird"—two attributes I had been perfectly comfortable with until I reached secondary stage, where sheep-mentality was the only acceptable way to be. But my mother persuaded me to go halves with her. The next day, a boy who had only ever shouted insults at me tried to find something rude to say as I walked by feeling self-conscious, but all he could think of muttering disappointedly was, "cool coat." Life got a bit better from then on.

Shopping with my parents was such a rarity that ironically the concept only became more alluring.

In my teenage years before I got a job, with limited pocket money, I trawled charity shops, antiques markets, and fairs to find treasures.

According to others, these items were strange, but I will list some and let you decide. There was

a pair of long-haired sheepskin yeti boots, an electric-blue cropped knitted tunic with a faux-fur hood and no sides, its front and back panels fastened with car seat-belt clips, a pair of men's curly-toed Indian slippers, the leather much too tough to make them wearable but beautiful nonetheless, and a huge free-flowing red dress with African tribesmen and women holding spears dancing all round it. It was a size 20 and I was a 6–8, but I had fallen in love with the print, and it was perfectly gatherable with a belt at the waist. I finally realised its flaw when the whole thing fell off onto the dancefloor at a party one evening.

Practicality never crossed my mind. They were as much curious and beautiful objects as they were clothing items. The challenge of curating them into looks was the ultimate pleasure—something Lyndell Mansfield's mother encouraged her to do, helping her experiment with who she wanted to be, without question.

ABOVE
Belinda "Bindy" Lambton, aka "Butterfly Lady," wearing her black velvet Henry VIII outfit (the one she asked to be buried in) and her butterfly hat, holding Violet's younger brother, Edley Naylor-Leyland, at his christening.

Similarly, unlike my school friends who often had to sneak miniskirts into handbags on a Saturday night, not once did my mother or father tell me to go back upstairs to change. They simply enquired quizzically about my attire over cocktails, deliberated on whether an item was indeed a skirt or a belt, then waved me off.

Charlie Casely-Hayford seemed to have a more enlightening experience, with his fashion-industry parents expertly critiquing each article of his eveningwear and explaining its significance in sartorial history, before their teenager walked out the door.

It was not until years later that my mother admitted to having taken her sisters and friends up to my bedroom while I was out, for regular wardrobe viewings. She described scenes of "rolling around the floor" and "crying with laughter." I was not offended by this tale. On the contrary, the shock and amusement my odd taste gave to others was an experience I found strangely enjoyable. Though this pleasure was inadvertently given, I loved hearing Andrew Logan say that his artwork and life were all about "bringing joy to the world."

There was someone in my family who sounded similar. As a small child, I only knew her as Butterfly Lady. She was in fact my maternal grandmother, Belinda "Bindy" Lambton. There were butterflies on her handbags, hats, dresses, jumpers, nighties, jewellery, shoes, and even her tights. She had butterfly tableware, lampshades and curtains, and her fitted bedroom carpet had a blue and white butterfly pattern across it. They might as well have been real, in my memory, fluttering around her, because the joyful atmosphere she created with this obsession was magical, as were the legendary anecdotes surrounding her theatrical imagination.

At Nicky Haslam's "The Hunt" themed fortieth birthday party held at his Hunting Lodge in Hampshire, Bindy arrived in a rubber frogman suit, complete with flippers and a speargun. To boot, having related this story to someone at a party a few years ago, I found out that she had travelled down on the train from Durham in this outfit as he had discovered himself in the same carriage as her.

When she died in 2003, I was given some of her more unusual possessions, as my mother and aunts decided I was the relation most likely to appreciate them. I often feel my happiest in her black silk corseted dresses or holding one of her butterfly bags. They instil a thrill and mischievous spirit I cannot help but channel.

Three years earlier on the eve of the millennium, after leaving school, I moved in with my grandmother on the King's Road in Chelsea, where the butterfly carpet was. One day, in a pub with some friends, I bumped into the stylist and style icon Isabella Blow. She was wearing a strange hat, had red lipstick on her wonky teeth and I thought she was mesmerising. She remarked on my unusual style and then a few weeks later offered me work experience. At her home in Waterloo, there were Alexander McQueen corsets hung

OPPOSITE
Violet in one of her grandmother's label-less dresses reminiscent of the Dior Bar Suit. It may in fact be Dior or a copy. We'll never know …

BELOW
A favourite item—a felt-lined decoupage butterfly handbag left to Violet by her grandmother.

on rails and giant coffee-table tomes on fashion and art all around. She introduced me to millinery via Philip Treacy, as well as modern art and the fashion industry. I died and went to heaven, metaphorically. With her encouragement, I became a stylist.

The worlds that these true originals, Issie and Butterfly Lady, curated around themselves via their clothing, interiors, and things they collected were weird, wonderful, asymmetrical, imperfect, deeply personal, and reflective of their lives full of inspirations, niche knowledge, tragedy, and comedy. I felt honoured to have been let in, and although they are now both gone, the memories and the magic have never left me.

I wanted to bring some of the wonder alive again by way of this book, so the one thread that had to bind those included here was an instinctive trend-flouting attitude that kept them doing things their way—something increasingly elusive these days.

Having been a writer, observer, and dresser of people for many years, I have learnt there is a unique story behind everyone, but the more unusual their taste, often the more interesting the tale, and the more I am lured by them.

I knew a few of the individuals featured in this book already, some I had admired closely for years, and others from afar. Yet nothing could prepare me for the charm, intrigue, and delight I felt being given the freedom to go behind closed doors, open drawers, nose around dressing tables, and delve into wardrobes to help them pick out beloved outfits to be photographed in, and witness this individuality echoed in their interiors and treasured collections. This was truly an aesthetical storytelling treat.

So, without further ado, I hope you enjoy getting lost in their worlds as much as I did.

VICTORIA GRANT

THE GENTLEMAN DRESSER

"DO YOU THINK I'm eccentric?" Victoria asks sincerely. She is referrring to how others have described the way she dresses.

I don't. I think the label sells short her true-to-self, well-thought-out, and beautifully-executed-style. But I am perhaps a little defensive about the word, which has often been thrown my way and struck me as a somewhat dismissive means of drawing attention to something strange or unconventional, done without rhyme or reason. Yet, what might be inexplicable to one person, can seem quite natural to another, with very often adequate reason, thought, or even sometimes poetry behind it. The observer just has not got to know it yet.

But perhaps she just asked the wrong person.

The word certainly becomes more appealing once you know that it derives from the astrological term "orbital eccentricity," referencing how much the orbit of an object deviates from a perfect circle. It strikes me that while perfect circles are indeed impressive, there are many more interesting and beautiful shapes in nature. Victoria, with her wild platinum blonde bouffant, tamed with clips and a headpiece above an acutely tailored three-piece-suit, is one of them.

Orbiting the Grant family dining-room table in the old Surrey market town of Farnham, where Victoria grew up, was an impressive collection of military hats from around the globe. The antiquary of these unusual items was her father, Michael, a former Pikeman and Musketeer. Frequent trips into London were made to see the Trooping of the Colour and the Key Ceremony at the Tower of London. "We always went to see the royal pageantry in the streets. So I grew up beside my dad in his coat and tassels, watching with sparkly eyes, all this pomp and ceremony," Victoria remembers.

On one recent special occasion, Victoria accompanied him to the headquarters of the Honourable Artillery Company in London. He was in full military garb and she wore her Britain Rocks headpiece, comprising a navy felt beret layered with white felt strips and red Petersham ribbon to form a Union Jack. Along the ribbon was a delicate crystal chain running towards a tiny central doll's-house-sized crown on top. Victoria tells me: "There was a moment when I was standing one glass of champagne away from the Queen, who looked up at my hat and gave me a smile."

In the same way a cowboy is rarely without his boots, Victoria naturally never leaves home without her hat.

A memory from aged fourteen of the moment style started to mean something, holds complete clarity for her. "There was this pair of trousers I saw in Morgan on Guildford High Street, and fell in love with. They were black with tiny rainbow flowers all over. I talked about them, drooled over them … They monopolised my life for about six months." Unable to afford them, Victoria assumed her plight had fallen on deaf ears, but someone had been paying attention.

Leonard Stanley Fearnley, Victoria's maternal grandfather, cut a striking figure in a white suit, panama hat and cravat with a giant aquamarine jewel around his neck. He had watched Victoria create from a young age.

ABOVE
A Victoria Grant leopard-print felt top hat displayed on a vintage Louis Vuitton vanity case.

PAGE 12
Victoria in her sitting room, cartwheeling in her own beret and favourite Mark Powell houndstooth three-piece suit.

OPPOSITE
Shower curtains are for dummies, especially when you have sequin headpieces and your mother's feather necklaces to adorn your bath instead.

FOLLOWING SPREAD
The master bedroom on a mezzanine balcony, just below the beautiful Victorian ceiling cornice, is grand and cosy in one glance.

"He had eccentric style," she says. And his interest in her clearly had an impact, for at the age of seven, Victoria put together a portfolio of fashion and interior creations she planned to turn into a business named All-sorts Designs after the colourful British confectionary Bassett's Liquorice Allsorts—her grandfather's favourite sweet.

By day, Victoria attended Frensham Heights, a boarding school near Farnham, an hour from London. It was renowned for its alternative traditions and open-minded approach to pupils, with a notable list of artistic British alumni including Pink Floyd drummer Nick Mason, comedian Jack Dee, actress Hattie Morahan, and author and illustrator Charlotte Hough. Teachers were known by their first names. There was no uniform, giving pupils room to express their individuality from an early age. Victoria looks back at one pair of jeans she wore aged thirteen, that were "ripped from cheek to cheek" and beneath which she styled men's form-skimming Calvin Klein underpants. "We would smoke fags and climb trees in the woods, with my bum completely showing. I can't believe I was allowed to go to school like that!" Victoria exclaims.

Diagnosed as dyslexic, Victoria found mainstream school academia, especially the literary kind, did not come easy, but by developing her own way of learning, her love of art and music flourished. Made to have piano lessons, she says: "I felt sorry for my teacher because I never ever practised—not once. She'd make me do sight-reading. I would say: "I just can't. I know the names of the letters, I know the notes. But I cannot read music." On the day before her Grade 1 piano exam, Victoria, not having practised, pleaded with her exasperated teacher to just play her the pieces. The next day, Victoria took the exam, performed from memory and passed. She managed up to Grade 4 using this method.

Her years at Frensham were full of artists' and rockstars' children, many of whose families had houses in central London or abroad. "They had these very exciting lives, that as the day-bug from a small country village I hadn't been exposed to. Their parents were really cool; they lived near the cool London shops and they had these whopping great allowances." Observing shopping trips to hip 1990s boutiques Hyper Hyper in Kensington and The Cross in Notting Hill, Victoria says, "Their style was a huge inspiration." But as her allowance was a more sensible "£30-a-month" to cover "everything from clothes to cinema trips," and having refused to wear a dress or skirt for as long as she could remember, creative ingenuity stepped in to fill the void in her purse, broaden her options, and become her saving grace in the school fashion stakes. "I couldn't afford what they had so I had to create my own look, by chopping, customising, and embellishing things" using her own wardrobe, charity shop or vintage market purchases to whip up these inventions. She saved up "for years" for a pair of patchwork flares from Hyper Hyper, which she paired with neon mesh tops and punk accessories from Camden Market. She describes herself in this early style phase as a "kind of cosmic, futuristic hippie, but always quite rock 'n' roll." She still wears the flares, and if she bumps into anyone from Frensham who she has not seen in years, they will often say "Oh wow, your style was so unique at school."

OPPOSITE
Victoria tickling the ivories in Café Royal's Oscar Wilde Lounge in a vintage cape, Temperley pussy bow blouse, and her own hat design.

FOLLOWING SPREAD
Two of Victoria's naughtiest hats; a black-and-white portrait of the milliner by Zoë Law; the designer's favourite Perrier-Jouët tipple; and Victoria's wonderful champagne bucket jungle on her Notting Hill balcony.

"
I WAS STANDING ONE
GLASS OF CHAMPAGNE AWAY
FROM THE QUEEN, WHO LOOKED
UP AT MY HAT AND GAVE ME
A SMILE.
"

When her grandfather Leonard took her shopping one Saturday to buy her the flares with rainbow flowers, Victoria felt understood. She explains: "Buying me those trousers was like him saying, 'I get you. I realise these are more to you than a pair of trousers. I believe you are going to design and do great things when you're older.'" The flares became a catalyst for the confidence she needed to pursue her dreams, and by buying these trousers, her grandfather had validated them. "You only need one cheerleader, don't you?" she says.

When her grandfather died, I am certain you can guess what she wore to his funeral …

Since I have known her, as the talented milliner and accessories designer who has made hats for Lady Gaga, Madonna, Rihanna, Dita von Teese, and the fashion brand Dolce & Gabbana, her mode has become more refined. She is less "cosmic hippie," more "chicly tailored sex-bomb … with a headpiece." Her array of perfectly tailored two- and three-piece suits from Joshua Kane, Mark Powell, and Gucci, structure and flatter her feminine frame, and the graphic prints, strong shapes, and rich fabrics she chooses for her clothes and accessory designs exude luxurious tangibility. The usually black-and-white or bright block-colour canvas acts as the perfect foil for her accoutrements: a hat, pocket watch, brooch or elaborately patterned neckpiece to add a "sting of colour" or poignancy to her look. "I love adding jewels to cravats or making interesting sculptural neck-shapes with scarves. The stiffening, draping, and sculpting of accessories and adornments gives you the opportunity to restyle your main wardrobe," she explains.

Her bespoke headpieces follow a similarly bold approach, and unable to find joy in muted colours, she even turned down a "beige" commission. Her hat names, such as Dark Horse, Lady Godiva, Lilac Wine, Peep Show, and Golden Shower, are about as far from beige as it gets. She uses sumptuous fabrics including velvets, wool, felt, fur, and feathers, as well as light-up neons featuring words like "Taxi," "Sex Shop," and "Girls Girls Girls." "I do love my neons. I haven't seen them anywhere else, and they create such a riot wherever they go," she says, anthropomorphising them as she does with all her hats—as if they were her children off on adventures of their own.

Her scarf collection would not look out of place in Keith Richards's wardrobe. Her electric, rock 'n' roll energy combined with a wicked sense of humour—a winning formula channelled into her design—makes Victoria herself irresistibly alluring. It is impossible to be in the same room as her and not want to come close to drink in the detail.

Eye-catching is her thing, for while styling windows at Coco de Mer, a luxury lingerie and erotica store in Covent Garden, selling 18-carat gold vibrators for £12,000, one pedestrian stopped to observe, and finally came in to get a closer look at the hats she was putting on. Completely engrossed in her job, Victoria had not noticed it was Daphne Guinness, the person whose style she admires above all others, trying on hats behind her. "The manager had been trying to eyeball me to go over and assist her," she says. After purchasing most of the hats she had just put up, Daphne, having effectively sabotaged her window display, offered, in her heel-less 7-inch Alexander McQueen platform shoes,

to climb up and redecorate. But by this point, Victoria was far from miffed about the decor.

Her own interior—a magical Notting Hill studio flat, with soaring high ceilings and elaborate Victorian cornices—pays perfect homage to this strong aesthetic. The floor is laid with a giant black-and-white geometrical patterned rug and the walls are covered in her colour-popping creations, photography, art, and neons. Looking up at the walls and then down at her outfit, she realises, laughing: "It's like looking in the mirror actually!"

Decor and personal style alike, what I love most about her dynamic is that, as well as the obviously pleasing aesthetics, there is poetry behind it too. The sharp, clean, defined elements make Victoria feel grounded and organised. A little vicarious army training seeping in perhaps? She says: "I need that structure, a clean, graphic solid foundation that I can then express creativity upon." And when she mentions that her mother made mosaics, jewellery, and painted tooth-fairy boxes that were sold at Harrods, the penny finally drops about how this wonderfully perfect creative storm was formed: "I get all of my artistry, resourcefulness, and creativity from my mum and my love of British pageantry and dressing up from my dad."

Yet she admits that the choice of a more traditional men's way of dressing and her dislike of high heels and dresses, also appeals to her childlike instincts: the little girl or rather little tomboy, who still wants to misbehave and climb trees. "I can't bear anything that's restrictive. I like to feel light and free. I want to be able to run, jump, and cartwheel in whatever I'm wearing." And stilettos would no doubt get caught in the foot pedals if playing a midnight rendition of "Let It Loose" by the Rolling Stones at The Groucho Club.

But best of all, she is honouring the dress code of the man who set her creativity free and perhaps, even, his Liquorice Allsorts.

OPPOSITE
A trip to Trafalgar Square isn't complete without some Temperley tailoring and Anna-Karin Karlsson sunglasses. And Victoria never leaves home without her hat.

LUKE EDWARD HALL

A THING OF
BEAUTY IS A JOY
FOREVER

WANDERING THE ROOMS of Luke Edward Hall and Duncan Campbell's Gloucestershire cottage, a perfume of newly picked sweet peas present, brought on some form of tactile-emotional synaesthesia—a rare syndrome (previously undiagnosed) whereby just the touch of something can bring on a strong feeling, or compulsion. I found myself in a frenzy of pointing to and picking up objects, cooing, asking what, where, and why. Everything was so beautifully placed, so inviting, it was impossible not to. I must have been the most annoying guest.

Each miniature bust or sculpture reminiscent of a Renaissance master, mounted tastefully on a smooth chunk of marble or painted plaster plinth, made me ache for the cobblestoned piazzas of Italy. A print of two muscular Greek nudes standing contrapposto brought on a pang of guilt at the memory of a classics teacher we tormented at school. I giggled at a gilt-rimmed ashtray from the Grand Hotel Quisisana, Capri, with thoughts of my own stolen treasures from fancy restaurants, visited as a teenager, in mind—no doubt theirs legitimately procured. On another plinth swirled with a marbleised pattern, sat a match box painted with the image of a long-haired and bejewelled Empress Elisabeth of Austria—uncannily, the reference I had used to inspire the hairstyle worn on my wedding day.

In the bathroom, I could not help but pick up a bar of almond soap from the Farmaceutica di Santa Maria Novella, a Florentine institution started by thirteenth-century Dominican monks, which my mother had introduced to me as a child. Trying to take in the delicate scent through the fawn paper reminded me of waiting patiently in the cool respite of the Tuscan pharmacy, gazing at the vaulted ceiling frescos, as no soap went unsniffed. On the same arsenic-green shelf the pink spotted tail of Lampedusa's Leopard seemed to be waving from a metallic Ortigia soap packet, sending my mind's eye across the sea to a Sicilian bar, where my husband and I, newly in love, sipped blood orange Bellinis and corralled bags full of lime di Sicilia and melograno soap under the table with our feet.

Opening Luke's wardrobe, was like delving into an Evelyn Waugh novel: double-breasted linen suits in lilac, green, and wide white pinstripes; and waistcoats in whimsical prints (all his own design)—one floral, another depicting a medieval hunting scene of hounds chasing hares with a wild boar climbing the collar to safety.

But then a flash of wild 1980s print hit my eye, a splat of red embroidery leapt out as I leafed through shirts, and a buckled corner of stonewashed denim stamped with a Californian bear iron-on patch showed its incongruity. The electric-blue satin Loretta Caponi pyjamas were another lavish surprise. And oh, the knitwear drawer: loud checks, fat stripes, and multicolour harlequin diamonds—it was like a David Hockney dream, but better! At the bottom of the stairs by the door sat matching pairs of Moroccan velvet slippers: one mustard yellow, the other emerald green. Looking through the door out onto a lawn backed with cow parsley lining a willow fence, there were pink and green tartan rugs set with pepper tarts on amber plates decorated with the sea god Neptune, pink peonies bursting from a tiny vase, rosé in a wicker basket, and a rolling view of the Cotswolds beyond. It was in this moment I realised my mind was fully in the present, engrossed in Luke Edward Hall's idyllic and wonderful world of style.

PAGE 28
Luke in a favourite vintage knit on his staircase at home in Gloucestershire.

OPPOSITE
Drawing should always be done in electric blue silk Loretta Caponi pyjamas.

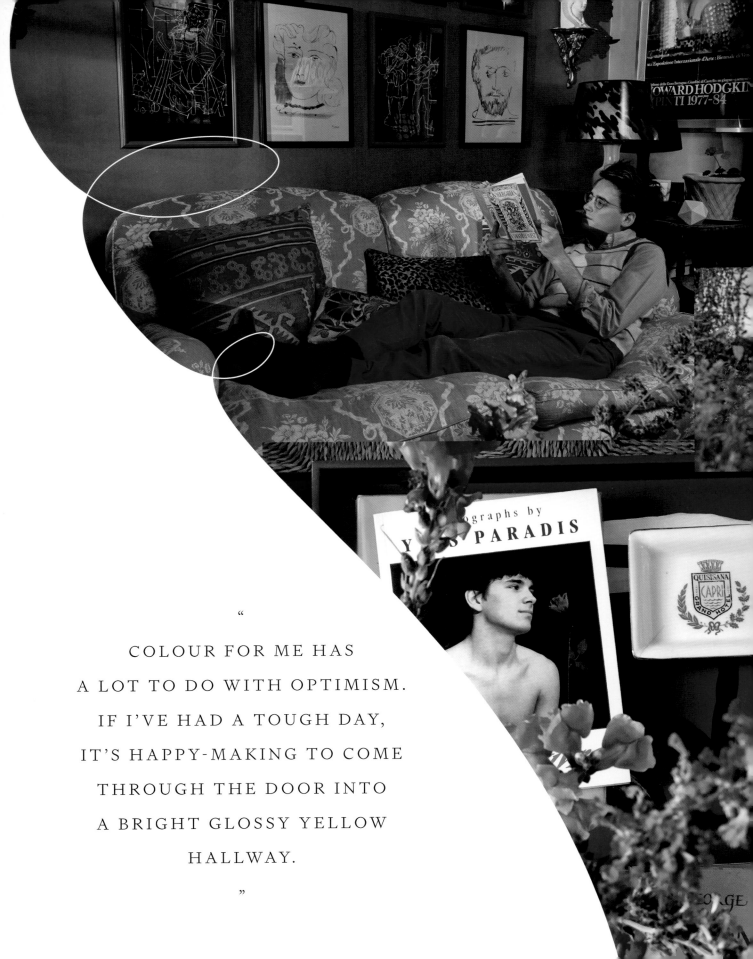

"

COLOUR FOR ME HAS
A LOT TO DO WITH OPTIMISM.
IF I'VE HAD A TOUGH DAY,
IT'S HAPPY-MAKING TO COME
THROUGH THE DOOR INTO
A BRIGHT GLOSSY YELLOW
HALLWAY.

"

IT'S ABOUT MIXING
THINGS UP AND CLASHING THEM
TOGETHER—TAKING SOMETHING OLD
AND INFUSING IT WITH
SOMETHING NEW.
"

Sorry to appear insistant , but
I must have my trinkets.   This is the last
chance.

THE CASTLE OF T
REST SAUVA

ENDYMION

ANNA THOMASSON

A Curious Friendship

The Story of a
Bluestocking and a Bright
Young Thing

PREVIOUS SPREAD
*The dining room, where
Luke likes to draw. He had
just bought the ornamental
painted wall plinth resting
on the table, from a small
local auction, and was
wondering where to put it.
He has painted leopard
spots on the candle holders
and the matador paintings
are by his hand, too.*

BELOW
*A miniature of a whippet
spotted hanging on the
kitchen wall.*

OPPOSITE
*The potting shed, a
favourite spot. Luke is in
one of his own waistcoat
designs made from vintage
fabric with a trellis print.*

FOLLOWING SPREAD
*An idyllic scene from
an Evelyn Waugh novel
to match the perfect
Gloucestershire view
beyond the wicker fence.
Luke, a wonderful cook,
made the tarts; the wine
glasses are by Campbell-
Rey, Duncan Campbell's
interior design company;
and the rosé in the wicker
basket came from next-door
Daylesford Organic. Luke's
double-breasted summer
suit is a charity shop gem.*

the moon goddess and tragedy ensues. It begins "A thing of beauty is a joy forever . . . " Luke explains. "I'd always been interested in storytelling, the Egyptians, Greek, and Roman mythology, legends and folklore." His collection campaign featured a wistful-eyed boy with a woven-willow crown wearing colourful knitwear: textures and patterns associated with the English countryside. "I am a knitwear fiend," he says. The drawings are artworks, the story inspiring them full of romance, and his collection was given a write-up on *Dazed Digital* in 2012.

In between studies, he worked with fledgeling Scottish fashion designer J.W. Anderson—now a global brand—and also at *Dazed* magazine with style director Nicola Formichetti, who is now, among other things, part of Lady Gaga's fashion design team at the Haus of Gaga. At weekends Luke worked in a Brick Lane vintage shop, and as a side project he started an online antiques business, Fox and Flyte, with Duncan and their best friend, selling items such as "1920s-inspired cocktail shakers and glassware, found at markets or on eBay," which they styled cleverly for photographs. "I always loved forming little businesses," he says. It was during this endeavour that he met British architect Ben Pentreath, who took him on to work at his design firm in the interiors department.

I asked why, after four years of studying fashion, he gravitated towards interiors. "I loved drawing, styling, and creating stories, but I hated making clothes. I was really bad at it, as I got older, I realised the fashion world, at least in the full-time sense, was not for me." Influenced by classical architecture, Pentreath's portfolio provided the perfect backdrop to the mythological stories Luke had fallen in love with, and after two years he felt the itch to start up on his own. "I loved working for Ben, but in the back of my mind I knew that I would always want to work on a lot of different projects, a bit of fashion, a bit of interiors, and my own artwork too, and somehow join all the dots between."

And joining the dots is what Luke does so brilliantly and with such imagination, gathering all that he enjoys best in life and with sleight of hand—or seemingly so—marrying them up into an artwork, design, or even an outfit. Look at anything Luke puts his hand to—whether it is chalk drawings on paper, paintings on ceramics, a flower or table arrangement—and you are not only taken to a lovelier place but also reminded of bygone eras where the people are glamorous, the living carefree, and the quest for beauty is at the very heart. Yet amid the references to the past, through his unconventional use of colour and juxtaposition of style, your eye is drawn by its newness and quirks. "I like to take inspiration from different places. There are the people I look up to—Cecil Beaton, Stephen Tennant, Rex Whistler, and Oliver Messel. And while reading about Ancient Greece I might also be listening to 1980s pop music. It's about mixing things up and clashing them together—taking something old and infusing it with something new."

The Luke Edward Hall signature style manages to conjure up all that is beautiful, inspiring, and optimistic about this world, reminding one of being in love, travelling, good food, music, and warm weather. It is so refreshing to dip into his world—a place that is also difficult to tear yourself away from, without, at least, a little souvenir.

LULU GUINNESS

BUNCHED!

RAPUNZEL'S TOWER, the red pagoda, her closet of skeletons, the Schiaparelli lobster dress, Madeline, Tara, a curly-locked Westie with a polka-dot bow, and those iconic red lips …

Woven through the designs of Lulu Guinness's bags is the tale of an extraordinary life of unique style and taste, wit and fun, bravery, love, and inspiration.

But when I ask Lulu what she would like to be photographed wearing for this book, she does not seem keen—in a sort of "been-there-done-that" kind of way—on the idea of clothes. I am stumped.

Moments later a picture pings onto my phone. It is a Moschino catwalk model in a gown with flowers bursting out from the top. "I don't even really see it as a dress," she says. Aha! We are finally on the same page. And how to do it? Well, it seemed straightforward to her—there was a large roll of art paper she had been meaning to use up, she loved arranging flowers, I was a stylist, her partner an art teacher … et voila: "Bunched" by Lulu Guinness!

Discovering she was "very small but with a tiny waist" growing up during the 1970s and 1980s, the prevailing hippie chic then "Calvin Klein natural girl with blond hair and jeans" trends, she found, did nothing for her. "I preferred everything my Granny wore to what my mother was wearing," she remembers, and she was "always very lured by glamour": the silver-screen, attention-grabbing type. Discovering Notting Hill's Portobello Market in her teens, with a "tenner" in her pocket she would leaf through the street rails, heading home with carrier bags bulging with 1940s crêpe du Chine tea dresses that cost her about £1.70 each. "It was all we had to spend," she says.

Despite being one of five granddaughters, as the only one interested in their wardrobes, when both grandmothers died, Lulu was given the pick from their beautifully tailored 1940s and 1950s figure-framing, waist-nipping cache. Her maternal grandmother, Betty Cohen, who had come from a line of Jewish retail heiresses, "was extremely stylish though in a conventional way" and had all her clothes made by London couturiers, whereas her other granny, Nesta Rivett-Carnac, had lived in Shanghai and left exquisite Chinese treasures unlike anything Lulu could find in British shops. A "shocking-pink evening jacket" is emblazoned in her memory.

Born Lucinda Jane Rivett-Carnac, the eldest of three with two younger brothers, she describes her family as "a bit of a mixture." Her father was Sir Miles Rivett-Carnac, 9th Baronet, a naval admiral and later CEO and chairman of international investment firm Barings. Her mother was April Villar, a Jewish Liverpudlian retail heiress whose family at one point owned Selfridges. Due to her father's military position, Lulu lived in Malta, Malaysia, and Singapore until the age of six, when the family returned to England.

The noisy splendour of Chinese New Year's dancing red and gold dragon processions and ceremonies formed many of her most vivid first memories. She remembers being fascinated by mah-jongg, a game (from the Qing dynasty, looking like a cross between dominos and playing cards) that a Chinese couple they lived with often played, and she wore few clothes due to the heat. I am charmed by a 1965 photograph of Lulu in her fifth birthday party outfit, which consists of a grass skirt, pink leis around her neck, wrists, and

PAGE 46
Turning Lulu into an arrangement using flowers from her garden and the Country Garden Florist was pure creative joy, even on the hottest day of the year. Isn't she sensational?

OPPOSITE
A view through a bed of roses of Lulu standing in her room in a dress from Thailand and Loeffler Randall shoes. Note the exquisite antique rose fabric on the inside of her four-poster pelmet—all the better for gazing up at.

ABOVE
The automated Lulu Guinness Birdcage Bag.

FOLLOWING SPREAD
Gothic arched windows in Lulu's sitting room look out onto a sweeping field of sheep tended to each day by a shepherd—but she feels they are her own now. I particularly loved the length of "Ms. Bo Peep's" curtains and the fact that many interior items are not necessarily where they ought to be—and to great effect.

ankles, and a tropical flower behind her ear. I ask whether the party had been themed but she explains this was not really considered "dressing up." "It wouldn't have been as big a step [sartorially] as it was if you lived in England … We never really wore shoes."

Making up for this barefootedness, twenty-one years later she wore her kitten heels on honeymoon to climb the Great Wall of China. She admits, "I was a never a paired-back plain kind of person." With regard to her personal style she says: "I like decorative, was always obsessed with embroidery, a little panel—anything with *work* on fascinated me." In her teens, she would layer five necklaces on top of one another, as well as wearing enormous costume jewellery earrings, but after moving to Paris she became aware of "the edit." Lulu embarked on a La Varenne cooking course to please her mother, acted in Noël Coward plays, and did a bit of "face-modelling." Surrounded by make-up artists, stylists, creatives, and a photographer boyfriend, she began to absorb the typically French less-is-more approach to style and how to "make a centrepiece of something and not have everything everywhere." She also realised how important it was "to dress to suit yourself" and not just piggyback every passing trend, as different trends suited different people.

Along the way, Lulu sampled punk, wore Italian designer Fiorucci, and danced at Palace nightclub on the Avenue des Champs-Élysées—the fashion crowd's epicentre. Just as I was wondering if she had sported a mohawk, she says: "It was all very *Parisienne* in those days—the capital of fashion … Our heroines were incredibly glamorous in comparison to the gritty reality of the English ones." She avoided the sporty look, refused to wear jeans, and thanked God for the arrival of high glamour, Grace Jones, Jerry Hall, *Vogue* fashion illustrator Antonio Lopez (who curated and captured much of this glossy drama) and above all "DISCO!" She says the word with such happy gusto I am almost blown over. But I can see why. It was a trend she could finally embrace and—far beyond anything else—it was fun, something Lulu felt was missing from much of the fashion industry.

She became a wiz at Paris vintage shopping and putting together looks that mixed new with old. With her dark hair, big round eyes, and perfect doll-like pout painted with "movie glamour" red lipstick from stage make-up stores, she began to coin a look that was very much her own. "It's part of my creative madness that I had to be different. I never wanted anything that anyone else had got. Gosh, I've calmed down a lot," she laughs.

Marrying Valentine Guinness, a descendant of the Irish brewing family, in 1986 at Winchester Cathedral Lulu wore an incredible peau de soie 1950s-style wedding dress and had a nineteen-year-old Daphne Guinness, Valentine's sister, as one of her bridesmaids. Three years on, fed up with working for others, she felt the itch to start something herself and in 1989 designed the Lulu Bag, a seemingly simple, black, soft leather briefcase that opens to reveal a violet velvet lining and a glut of secret pockets and compartments. It was but a glimpse of the magic and delight she was destined to create. Finding it initially odd that people asked if she had designed not only the bag she was carrying but also

OPPOSITE
Lulu is often found in her wellies and vintage kimono, and her kitsch striped umbrella can be seen as you drive up the hill from the picturesque village below.

FOLLOWING SPREAD
Some artwork by Lulu; a Rex Whistler collector's item; porcelain playing cards; an extraordinary bust, silhouetted by a window; and a dining room cabinet of curiosities displaying antiques, Lulu Guinness bags, and a Katrin Moye jug vase.

> "
> I WAS ALWAYS VERY LURED BY GLAMOUR.
> I PREFERRED EVERYTHING MY GRANNY WORE TO
> WHAT MY MOTHER WAS WEARING.
> "

the outfits she was wearing, it finally dawned on her that her style, taste, things she collected and said, even her interiors choices and bedlinen were all part of the package. And so, Lulu's world became the brand. "People bought into my world. And you've seen my world. And I can't help it. My daughters are always saying I have too many things."

Even her approach to design gave her a unique edge in the industry. Regarding her original ambition to design stage sets, she says: "I always liked objects. I never saw myself as a bag designer, just an object designer—then I started carrying it," she says.

Over the last three decades Lulu's portable creations have included the Florist Basket, a black satin bucket filled with red roses; an evening dress with a liftable skirt flap, underneath which is embroidered "Lulu caught you looking," a bag with a hidden camera in it; and countless versions of her fabulous lips. She has collaborated with artists, embroidered a tote with the Queen of Hearts for Helena Bonham Carter, produced an ode to heroine Elsa Schiaparelli's lobster gown, and one of her finest creations—her automated Birdcage, with singing bird inside, is now in London's Victoria and Albert Museum. Her designs are stylish, fun, clever, and punchy—right on brand.

Lulu gave birth to two daughters, Tara in 1991 and Madeline in 1997, and encountered two severe bouts of postnatal depression, which were followed by a diagnosis of bipolar disorder. Despite this struggle, she still continued to inspire, create, and achieve. She split from Valentine in 1999, remaining friends and living next door to one another to bring up their children together. In 2005, she wrote a book with Rizzoli, *Put On Your Pearls, Girls!*, full of witty advice to inspire the modern glamour girl, with secret pull-out-pages and lift-up flaps galore. The sage guidance includes, "If you want to be drop-dead gorgeous—be a Hitchcock heroine for the day!," "You *CAN* be too rich or too thin," and "Follow your heart … And life will be a bed of roses." In 2006 Lulu received an OBE for services to the fashion industry and in 2009 *The Independent*'s Lifetime Achievement Award in Handbag Design.

Continuing to inspire, when I visit her Gothic folly in Stroud, the dining table is laid out with illustrations she has been working on for a stationery company and her house is filled with captivating objets d'art: an ironwork crown of stars hung over the staircase, Staffordshire china sheep perched on the windowsill peering out at the real flock beyond, a gargoyle face on a book illustrated by Rex Whistler that reveals another face when rotated, and an enviable collection of hand-painted Katrin Moye vases. Her eye for intrigue and curiosity is incomparable. "Oh, this is only a fraction of it!" she says. I imagine that this is the same for her ideas—endless. "I have lots of other worlds. This is just the one I'm into at the moment."

As my mind wanders to these exciting other worlds that I hope someday to encounter, I notice how serene she seems in the one she is in. Dressed in a green vintage silk kimono and wellington boots, the hose is turned on and on this very hot day, she must water her roses.

"
I NEVER SAW MYSELF
AS A BAG DESIGNER, JUST AN
OBJECT DESIGNER—THEN
I STARTED CARRYING THEM.
"

BEATA HEUMAN

IN AN OLD
FARMHOUSE IN SWEDEN...
ALL COVERED WITH TILES

TWO SALT-RIMMED MARGARITAS were sipped, the first deftly removed by the slender hand of her husband, John Finlay, and replaced with a newly frosted glass. And while nursing my mint tea and reflecting on my own soon-to-be-improved marital habits, Beata mused, eyes twinkling, over the style of the 1930s. "The clothing was so well-made, the cut of things … a sleeve with buttons … the dresses … it was just so elegant. I wish someone would start cutting clothes like that again." I am in agreement.

Beata Heuman, "B," is one of my closest friends, and while I could happily meander in chat with her for hours, I am aware for the first time in our fifteen-year friendship that I must just listen, and try to see her with the fresh eyes needed to introduce her to you properly by way of this wonderful book.

Some unconventional choices in her diction, a little extra air under each vowel and perhaps another millisecond spent on her s's, are just enough to raise suspicions of a different, perhaps more formal English education, but otherwise, it is not easy to pinpoint her Scandinavian roots. Although she learnt English at school in Sweden, she is often mistaken for a British aristocrat: an accent that may have trickled in via the Charles H. Cecil Studios' painting school students whom she befriended during her formative post-school year in Florence. She finds this mistaken identity curious yet does not mind it, but thoroughly objects to being called a Sloane.

Beata and her three siblings—older brother Felix and sisters Ebba and Keira—grew up at Sireköpinge farm, in the south of Sweden, where her father, Hans Heuman, grows wheat for Swedish vodka brand Absolut. Both her parents received doctorates in medicine but only her mother, Kristina, continued on in the profession, as a lung specialist, while her father's career turned to agriculture.

"Growing up in the countryside in the middle of nowhere, it didn't matter what you wore much. I was used to wearing my siblings' old clothes," Beata remembers, but also recalls a distant resentment about the "Minnie Mouse sweat pants" her kindergarten peers wore, which her parents refused to buy her. Instead, she had to make do with her brother's "old orange corduroy trousers"— an aesthetical deprivation for which perhaps she can now be grateful.

Although it took her until recently to appreciate the subtleties of her parents' way of dressing, not always understanding her mother's style and even being embarrassed by it as a child, she concurs: "I now think she's kind of a genius." On Beata's wedding day her mother wore a morning suit when walking her daughter down the aisle—a role her father had rejected on feminist grounds. (At Swedish weddings, traditionally the bride and groom walk into the church together, but Beata, marrying Englishman John Finlay, wanted to inject some English tradition into her day, although by swapping roles her parents rather threw a spanner into the works.) Beata had written Hans off, too, as a wardrobe dunce, but after noticing that most of east London modelled themselves on his dress sense, she realised in fact that he had turned out to be a "total hipster."

Wondering what the local trends were like in 1990s Skåne, I ask whether there was anyone else who inspired her growing up and she insists that, other than her maternal grandmother who made her own

PAGE 61
Beata in front of the headboard she made by mounting and bordering a throw for the bedroom she and her husband, John Finlay, share in Hammersmith. The glimpse of a necktie is from her Emilia Wickstead blouse worn beneath a vintage duster she bought in Florence.

OPPOSITE
Reading to daughter Alma in a bespoke Bode corduroy suit painted with lobsters and the names of her two children. The mural was copied from Bemelmans Bar at the Carlyle Hotel in New York.

1950s gowns, "honestly it was rather dismal round my parts." In her early teens, to break the monotony of "group mentality dressing" at the local school, she would every so often feel the need to do something "unexpected and a bit *off*, but not in a way that was too in your face … to keep them guessing," she remarks. "I liked to play with the tension of that. It's a little bit the same with my interiors." Going to school in her mother's old 1970s clothing was just the ticket. "I really liked that people were looking at me because I wore something different."

But shortly after her arrival at boarding school Beata gave in to peer pressure and, just wanting to fit in, followed a trend inexplicably foreign to her. Framing her brow with her free hand, in a mock attempt at shielding her eyes from the memory of "Lacoste polo shirts and fake Louis Vuitton bags," it is clear this recall is painful. "Actually, perhaps most other people had real ones … Either way, I lost myself style-wise a bit during that time," she laughs.

Dainty feet was another regrettable school trend, which Beata sampled, squishing her "size 39s" into size "35 shoes," something I explained my grandmother had inflicted on my mother as a child, whimsically regarding Chinese foot binding as "romantic." But as Beata rightly points out, "There's nothing romantic about a bunion."

Freed from the institutional constraints that made unusualness unpopular, at age nineteen she left school bound for Italy, where her sister Ebba studied painting and where Beata hoped to learn the language. Socialising with an arty and international crowd, amid the incredible Renaissance art, museums, and palazzi of Florence, she let loose her creative expression again, teaming her otherwise "conservative" wardrobe with things that were "unexpected and a bit weird." She modelled for the art school for extra cash. "Any nude?" I ask. "Too prude," she says. And she temporarily joined a band called the Animal Rescue Unit, as "the backing vocals." Although her dreams of fluent Italian were not perfectly realised, she feels the misspent hours romanticising over art and architecture among the predominantly English-speaking art students and teachers laid the foundations for her education and interest in the subject. It was these "cool folk from London town," who inspired her to make the English capital her next stop and later on home.

After moving into a flat in Chelsea with her then English boyfriend (former Animal Rescue Unit guitarist and my brother Tom), she was introduced through friends to interior designer, turbo-socialite, and fellow book entrant Nicholas "Nicky" Haslam, who, seeing potential, took her on at his design firm to learn the trade, and under whose wing she flourished for nine years before starting up on her own.

Nicky's style combined a deep knowledge, love of, and appreciation for traditional English interiors and classical architecture with a rule-breaker attitude that must have appealed to B's childhood sensibilities. Her fondness for him and admiration for his attitude to life and particularly his personal style comes across warmly. "He is amazing, open-minded, and fearless, and definitely loves to experiment." She describes office mornings when he would turn up in a "giant brown voluminous mohair cardigan with a moustache glued to his upper lip," or wearing a "beanie with hair sewn into the back," and "we weren't meant to bat

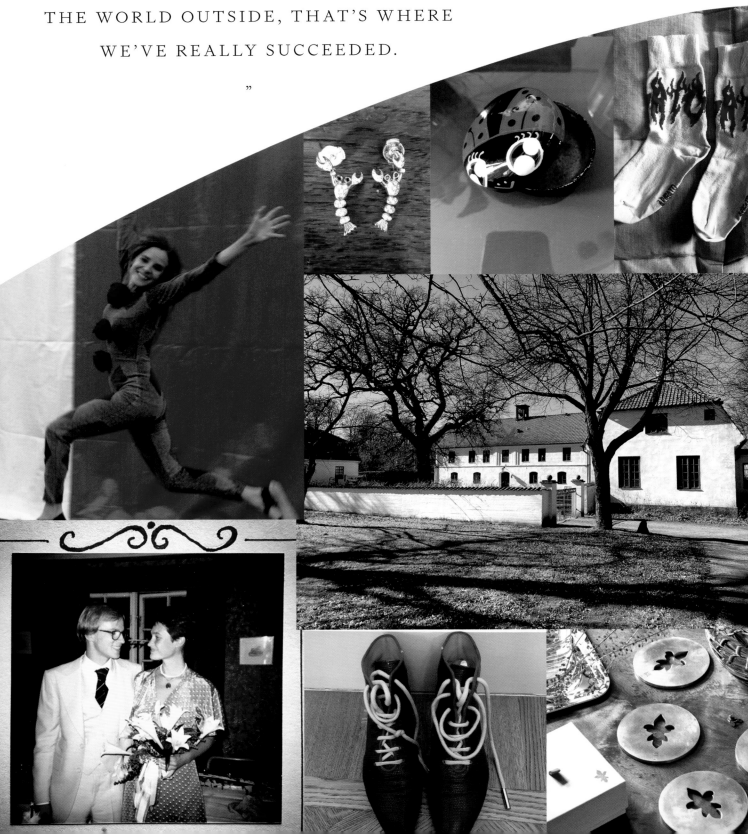

an eyelid." In reference to his sartorial approach, Beata feels she picked up a lot: "mainly that it's much more interesting when you stop caring what other people think and just do what you want; that's when you get something worthwhile and inspiring."

One of the things I love about B's style is that it is a mix of what she calls conservative (and I would label more Swedish ceramic student/farm gappie) linen overalls or jeans and a faded T-shirt with her father's farm company brand printed across it and what she admits is probably the comfort of "tapping into her twelve-year-old self." Just when you've grown comfortable with her in those outfits, she will surprise you by wearing a mustard-on-mustard Americana corduroy suit graffitied with lobsters, socks licked with flames, or a curious pewter lurex harlequin jumpsuit with oversized pom poms—her OOTD (outfit of the day) for lunch the day after her wedding.

This jack-in-a-box-type playfulness with her sartorial choices is all the better received amid the quieter wardrobe moments: a less-is-more until more-is-best approach … and then *boo!*

But even in her more understated ensembles, if you look a little closer you may catch a glimpse of some bespoke "Beata Heuman" marbleised lining inside her double-breasted navy Charlie Casely-Hayford suit jacket, a pair of red Charlotte Olympia lips pouting on her trainer toecaps poking out from the hems of her hand-me-down jeans, or a coral crayfish in one ear and a little gold and diamond arrow in the other.

In the same way that her interiors tap into the magic of storytelling, so does her style. Like Ludwig Bemelmans' *Madeline* picture-book illustrations of the 1930s, her style skips about between familiarity and surrealism, coming alive with the tale of a little Swedish girl on a farm who takes a trip through her mother's 1970s wardrobe, down the River Arno to Florence to play with artists and musicians, on to the bohemian society of London where she falls in love, over to New York with her debonair designer to drink martinis at the Carlyle Hotel bar, before jumping out of the pages and into the bedroom of her daughters, Gurli and Alma.

Every one of her stories is always worthwhile, and always inspiring.

ZANDRA RHODES

PRINCESS OF PUNK

WHEN YOU ARRIVE at Zandra's place you feel immediately foolish, not just for having consulted your map so many times, but for bothering to have looked at it at all. Amid the gin bars and sourdough pizza restaurants spilling from railway arches, Victorian shopfronts housing gluten-free bakeries and old industrial buildings turned into studios, smack in the middle of Bermondsey in London is a giant bright orange rendered cement box, spanning half a block, with a four-metre-high cerise pink door and high windows. This is the Fashion and Textile Museum. On the roof is another box—a matching pink with train-carriage-like windows running along the front and sides—this is Zandra's studio and home. You could have done no better than Ricardo Legorreta had you architecturally personified this lady yourself, the only thing missing, perhaps, is the blue eyeshadow. I wish I could have asked if this was what the late Mexican architect was thinking.

Inside the penthouse there is so much going on it is rather difficult to focus until you sit down and look around the room. Colour, textures, fabric, pattern, mirrors, artwork, sculpture, greenery, and most notably light permeates every retinal atom. There are giant painted wooden "Zs" to sit on, mosaic portraits of the owner balanced on vases, zigzag-patterned crockery hanging from the walls, and a life-size swan coated in pink glitter in one corner.

On the central table is a four-tiered fifty-holed Chinese finger vase diligently filled with yellow stems. There are flowering pot plants everywhere, many blooming dubiously early. "They encourage the real ones to come out," she says, which I believe for a second. Either side of the main southerly window overlooking the Bermondsey rooftop beehives is a pair of eight-foot Corinthian columns with fluted channels licked in gold, blue, and pink paint. On the one windowless wall painted an ombre white to orange, giant artworks by Andrew Logan, Duggie Fields, and Andrew Stahl are propped or hung. Mahatma Gandhi smiles down at you from one. On the surrounding roof terrace dusty pink delphiniums and lush tropical leaves flutter and sway through the windows. It feels like you have entered a Zandra Rhodes–themed psychedelic botanical greenhouse—all rather trippy.

Take any snapshot of the "Princess of Punk's" penthouse and you can pick out little details that are mirrored in the oversized ring or bracelet she is wearing, the particular shade of lipstick or haircolour she has chosen that day, but most of all in those eponymous prints she designs and wears.

"I do think I have a strong personal style. I don't know what it is. It's just me," says Zandra in a way that infers she might never have considered it. She remembers as a teenager being unable to use the loo because her pencil skirt was so tight. The only solution was to "take it off." I asked whether her style had changed much over the years and she remarks that since she started designing clothes in 1969, she has almost always worn her own pieces, although she admits, "Unfortunately now I have to expand the samples to fit." Sample-size she may not be, but nonetheless at eighty-one, she has a lovely figure and is a fine advertisement for her creations.

When we meet to photograph her, she wafts in wearing a floaty pink printed chiffon top and brick-red organza palazzo pants rippling above a comfy looking pair of fluorescent-pink trainers. A chunky beaded necklace designed by her friend Andrew Logan and a fuchsia-pink bob frame her open and wonderfully

PAGE 75
Zandra in a spectacular gown of her own design, watering geraniums on her roof terrace. She is a keen gardener and buys fake blooming plants in the winter to encourage the real ones to flower.

OPPOSITE
Zandra in an organza lamé Zandra Rhodes design sat in her Gandhi lounge with cushions from her previous homeware line. The mirrored artwork is by artist and friend Andrew Logan. She also wears some of his jewels.

FOLLOWING SPREAD
View through Zandra's studio with Andrew Logan's bust of the designer on the bannister; a striped Carole McNicol vase filled with exotic fake blooms, some extraordinary ceramics shaped like squashes and sea urchins and the familiar Zandra Rhodes silk cushion patterns on the sofa below. Her wonderful plate and teacup collection can be seen on the back wall in the kitchen.

PAGES 80-81
Regal Zandra at eighty-one years young, wearing a Zandra Rhodes pleated gown and Andrew Logan jewels, at her dining table with a hint of a pink glitter flamingo in the background.

"
I DO THINK I HAVE A STRONG
PERSONAL STYLE. I DON'T KNOW WHAT IT IS.
IT'S JUST ME.
"

won an Emmy). In her fiftieth year of design, she finished a collection of notepaper and cards for Museums & Galleries Ltd, signed a deal with Ikea, and created prints for Pierpaolo Piccioli at Valentino.

"Maybe if I'm very lucky something will happen like it did with Chanel or Schiaparelli: it didn't go that well when they were alive—it all came about afterwards," she says, referring to their success. At this point, I am not sure what to say to the Dame who has made clothes for "Lady Di" and Freddie Mercury, appeared as a cameo in British comedy series *Absolutely Fabulous*, and in 2019 received the Walpole British Luxury Legend Award. Surely she has surpassed cult-figure status and is now a household name?! But perhaps like beauty, success is within the eye of the beholder, and if you think you have made it, even after surviving fifty years in such a fickle industry, maybe that is when you give up.

Before we wave goodbye, Zandra gets geared up to go back to the studio and dons a brown suede builders' toolbelt I recognise as the same one my husband uses for manual work. As she clips in the plastic harness at the back and stuffs her frayed blue notebook into one of its well-worn pockets, for a shocking second I fear complacency has got the better of her and practicality has nudged style clumsily out of the way. When I look closer, however, I see it has been customised with minute multicoloured paint splashes and LOVE written with a Sharpie on the front panel. Fabulous!

OPPOSITE
Zandra's colour-coordinated bookcase of eclectic titles.

BELOW
The poster for Zandra's exhibition celebrating fifty years in fashion.

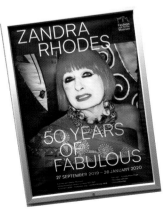

LYNDELL MANSFIELD

LADY
STARDUST

THROUGH THE MIST of hairspray and Chaka Khan playing on Brisbane radio, ten-year-old Lyndell sat on her mother's bed, watching her freshly dyed purple hair being "spiked up" for a night out. While a girlfriend squeezed into doll-sized stretch leggings, Ugg boots, and a flannel jumper, Lyndell's uncle threw on a cropped denim jacket above his bronzed stomach. "I was super lucky because my 'Ma' had this second phase of going out when I was ten, and that was such an influential time on a little girl," she says, harking back to the shamelessly kitsch world of 1980s Australian fashion.

Twenty years later and Lyndell Mansfield, one of Britain's most sought-after hairstylists, is at 33,000 feet, snipping hair for Michael Schumacher in a private jet. She is a regular feature on film sets coiffing Gwyneth Paltrow or backstage with Neneh Cherry, and *still* hangs out in bedrooms but this time those belonging to Joan Collins, Ivana Trump, Eva Herzigová and Roger Federer, around whose heads of hair she busies herself.

She has styled hair for most top international editorials including the cover of *10 Magazine Australia*— one of her proudest achievements—and become known for creating media-grabbing, career relaunching hairstyles for pop stars Paloma Faith, Jess Glynne, and Beth Ditto.

In Leytonstone, East London, if she is not in her red leather and feather-boa-upholstered home hair salon or sipping vegan cocktails in her pink plastic hot tub, she will be leafing through 1970s Scandinavian porn (for hairstyle inspiration). She becomes "Hairdresser on Tour" at Pikes Hotel Ibiza every year and runs a rock 'n' roll night in London every Thursday.

Besides being serious fun, wickedly humorous, sincere, and intuitive with an endearingly shy streak that *almost* prevented her appearing in this book (but for my insistence), she is at the top of her craft and everything your dream hairdresser ought to be. Her corkscrew mop of powder-pink curls can be spotted a mile off and she has a way of dressing that causes you to feel immediate joy and to sigh simultaneously at how cool she is.

Almost everything she owns is second-hand. "We couldn't afford *shit*, babe!" she says with an Aussie twang, referring to a childhood looking for furniture and clothes at the Salvation Army shops her mum worked in. She admits having grown used to "old metal frame beds with creaky springs" and "$2 clothing steals": this is just what she feels comfortable with. "I've been filling my house with that since I got my first flat at sixteen. And now it's trendy!" she laughs.

Her mother, Vivienne, considered opening a vintage store called V.W. hoping people would mistake it for a Vivienne Westwood shop, but in fact it stood for "Vivienne Who?" as she had been married so many times. "She had a thing for a man in uniform, so I was pretty much an army brat," Lyndell says. Her father had been in the navy and her "Pa," Vivienne's fourth husband, Barry, in the army. "When I was twelve, she found 'the one'—my Pa—and they're still together." As a result of constant travelling, by the time Lyndell was in her last year of education, she had been to more schools than there were school years, going back and forth between Sydney, Brisbane, Townsville, and Melbourne.

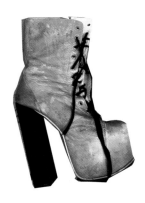

PAGE 94
Lyndell still reigns as coolest cat, resplendent in vintage leopard print, posing below one of her musical icons, Prince, whose leather-clad crotch is just visible.

ABOVE
Lyndell's seven-inch platforms.

OPPOSITE
The iconic customised leather jacket that hung at the bar at Lyndell's live music nights, DIY Thursdays (aka "Hole of Noise"), plastered with buttons she made for each night's theme and her motto "Because you can't stand around waiting for shit to happen." And she didn't …

FOLLOWING SPREAD
Lyndell and partner Tom's sitting room where David Bowie lyrics adorn the cushions and a 1984 Pirelli calendar hangs above the doorframe. Minty the (toy) cat stands guard near the light projector, VHS tapes and vinyl records.

Always the new girl, she became adaptable and made friends quickly, flitting between posses of goths, yuppies, punks, rude boys, rockers, and surfies. "I was the crossover kid—friends with all of them—piercing ears and cutting and colouring hair with felt-tip pens or food dye in the toilets," she explains. At high school in Brisbane, insistent on wanting to earn her own money, she asked her mother to help her lie about her age to get a "tea and tidy job" at a hair salon. Dutifully obliging, Vivienne got her twelve-year-old daughter into a salon where her best friend worked and was in on the deception. Every Saturday morning and Thursday night after school, she swept hair and made tea, and on Saturday afternoons and Sundays worked at a roller rink. After two years, she was offered a salon apprenticeship, but had to come clean that she was too young to legally accept until she turned fifteen.

Up until this time, Lyndell had excelled at school and had been offered art and drama scholarships, but with a busy life outside education, her academic interest was starting to wane, she was skipping classes and hanging out with older kids outside. Aware of her family history, she says tentatively: "No one had stayed in school, had an education or a trade and I didn't want to follow in their footsteps," but persuading her mother to let her leave was an obstacle more personal than she appreciated at the time.

At sixteen, Vivienne had been doing her hairdresser apprenticeship when she became pregnant with Lyndell and gave it up before she was born. "I think she didn't want me to meet a boy, get pregnant, and not finish my apprenticeship. I know that sounds horrible, but you do have that natural fear for your child, when it's happened to you, don't you?" Lyndell says.

Her admiration, respect, and understanding for her mother come across deeply. They sound similar in many respects, too, not least because Vivienne was a wiz at pulling rabbits out of hats. Undeterred by restrictions of military housing and disruptive relocations, she created worlds for Lyndell and her brother Darren to inhabit and fantasise in, building treehouses and tents in the garden, and sewing amazing fancy-dress outfits. "My mum was going through so much of her own personal stuff that she always put to the side, to make sure we didn't feel that," Lyndell remembers, and despite non-traditional artistic surroundings, she managed to create an environment for her children to be creative in. "I didn't understand I was into fashion as a kid. I just knew I loved imagery, movies, making scrapbooks and collages. I really *dressed* myself. She'd encourage me to wear all sorts."

Vivienne nurtured Lyndell's freedom to express herself and act out fantasises of being a boy and a girl without question. "I think I've always felt as feminine as I do masculine," Lyndell says, and with her mother's encouragement in experimenting with clothing, looks, and personas, she was able to start working out who she was, what she wanted to be, and how she would represent herself to the world. She says: "By the time I left high school I'd had long hair, short hair, bleached, shaved, and a chequerboard undercut, and because of her [Vivienne] we always won *all* the fancy-dress [competitions]."

PREVIOUS SPREAD
Lyndell and Tom's mix of retro second-hand furniture houses Lyndell's collections of dolls, silk scarves, erotic literature and prints, and some Japanese and burlesque fans. Tom's guitar is on the bed.

OPPOSITE
Lyndell sat in her home hair salon chair upholstered in 1960s red leather.

WHEN IT COMES TO MY INSTINCTS, I ALWAYS THINK,
THERE'S THE DOOR—IT'S OPEN. IF IT FEELS GOOD
TO ME, I'LL WALK THROUGH IT.

106

In the end, Lyndell's bid for a career won over Ma's maternal instincts. At sixteen she left school, rented a flat in Brisbane, and started to carve her path. By eighteen, earning only $100 a week with a $65/week rent to pay, she started working nights, dancing on podiums, as "the Hype girl" in "all the cool clubs." One night she was a sixties go-go girl and another she was lip-syncing as "Lady Marmalade." She also became involved in the production. "I used to choreograph thirty dancers, make their costumes, and sew their wigs," she describes this with such relish that it is clear her night shift was not just to fill the gap in her wallet, but a brilliant way of fulfilling her passion for music, dressing up, acting, and styling. "Dancer meets clown, so performer all round!" she quips.

While working in a "fancy salon" near the park, she often ate her lunch on a bench opposite an Aboriginal community who hung out there. One day a young girl from the group came up and pushed her to the ground, badly winding her. "It was weird; I didn't feel upset. I realised I must have made her feel uncomfortable," she says, and came back the next day to sit in the same spot. This time, one of the female elders approached and said to her: "You're one of us, aren't you? Don't worry, those girls won't come near you again."

Lyndell had only recently discovered her great-grandmother was Aborigine. She had marked "Māori" on her son's (Lyndell's grandfather's) birth certificate in the hope of giving him a better chance of employment in Australia. He was, in fact, half Aboriginal Australian, making Lyndell one eighth Aborigine.

Having known so little about these indigenous origins, going to the park to watch and listen to this group made her feel close to them. It was only when her grandfather died that she met her cousins and uncles, found out more about this part of her heritage and finally became part of the community.

At twenty-six, Lyndell's Australian hairdressing career was at the stage where she had "won awards and worked for amazing people." She was thinking of starting a school "to help indigenous boys and girls get into hairdressing" when she was invited to enter a major competition. The challenge was to produce haircuts on stage in front of an audience. The prize was a trip to a big hairdressing event, Salon International in London. "If you'd have asked me if I would move abroad and do my job I would've told you—absolutely no way! I *loved* Australia. I loved doing my job there." But as fate would have it, another relocation was in the cards. Lyndell worked her magic, on stage in front of a live audience, won, and off she went.

She booked for a few weeks' stay in London, and while visiting applied for a work visa on the off-chance she might stay longer. Opportunities arose that were beyond her dreams. She flew to Brigitte Bardot's Cannes house for a *Vanity Fair* shoot, to Paris to dye hair red for an Alexander McQueen show, and even made merkins for an arty 1970s-style LA shoot, putting her bedside reading to good use. "I would never have got to do that in Australia," she says.

But, sadly for Down Under, she fell for London—and for a wonderful musician called Tom—and made it her new home.

"I think that's the last time they gave that prize out," she says. I bet it was. But how lucky we were that they did.

NICKY HASLAM

ANYTHING GOES

AS A TWIG-MIMICKING stick insect or rainforest creature blending in among the dappled leaves, Nicky, the anti-chameleon of style, would do very poorly, gobbled up by predators in a flash.

Whether modern art with Gothic architecture, black leather among black tie or wit amid the mundane, he is a virtuoso of juxtaposition, unpredictability being the one thing you can count on.

I have always enjoyed looking out for him at parties, his absence merely confirmation of a more star-studded affair elsewhere. Part of the enjoyment of "Nicky-spotting" is watching him penetrate the eyeline of an elderly Sloane, who is choking slightly at his entrance in hip-skimming combat trousers, a camouflage-print T-shirt, and Paris Hilton or some flavour-of-the-month on his arm. While covering events for *Vanity Fair*, I was amused to see him hobnobbing with Hollywood royalty in jodhpurs and a tweed jacket, which was equally confusing for them too. Often you would find he had dressed for one particular soirée—lederhosen for a fancy-dress bash or Austrian engagement party perhaps—but being so in demand, might attend a book launch, *Tatler* party, and dinner at Annabel's before finishing there. Therefore, his dedicated outfit would be seen and enjoyed in some incongruous settings en route.

Nicky has been through more personal style phases than Elizabeth Taylor has had husbands: "head-to-toe-leather with bleached hair," "combat gear," "fashionably ripped jeans with pocket chains," "country tweed," "camel-coloured at-leisure wear, matching Converse and shaved head," "eighteenth-century jodhpurs," "double denim," "S&M," and a sort of "Oscar Wilde meets couture cowboy" are looks I have personally witnessed. No doubt there are more. But it is his inexplicable knack of pulling them off with such flippant sincerity that is so impressive.

One time I spotted him in black tie. Bowled over by this display of convention, I asked who he was wearing. "Philip Green, darling," he replied, and my thoughts of Saville Row faded as I realised he was referring to the retail tycoon whose company owned high-street store Topshop.

I ask why so mercurial. He says flatly: "I hate my looks. I'm completely unvain in that respect. I'd like to be the opposite of what I am. So my style reflects my alter ego—my longing to look like other people." And in the rich societal dance of the interior designer and socialite extraordinaire, "other people" have played a huge part.

You only need glance at the index in his memoir *Redeeming Features* (2009) to take in some of the extraordinary figures that have crossed his path, some now posthumous entries, many legends in their fields but all accompanied by wonderfully fascinating or funny stories.

He describes Min Hogg, founding editor of *The World of Interiors* magazine, a great friend, whose family Nicky stayed with near Regent's Park on exeats from Eton College, being the first to persuade him to bleach his hair for a night at Paris club Le Carrousel, much to his mother's annoyance.

The story of art collector Peggy Guggenheim taking him on boat trips through Venice, and round Vicenza in a limousine is quite a vision. Woody Allen lived in the flat below his apartment in New York although their only exchange was an apology from the comedic neighbour about his music taste.

PAGE 108
Nicky in his sitting room smoking and reading his most recent interiors project published in House & Garden. *He designed the sofa for the room, deciding it looked like one from a talk show. The flowers he arranged were stems sent from Luke Edward Hall's garden down the road.*

OPPOSITE
View through antique plates to a wax bust of seventeenth-century playwright Jean de Rotrou by Jean-Jacques Caffieri and a vase cleverly painted to look like marble.

FOLLOWING SPREAD
Nicky's cosy reading room with an almost sofa-length footstool. Mauny bamboo wallpaper provides the background for a selection of Nicky's watercolours.

EVERY
ROOM
SHOULD
SING

NICKY'S COWBOOT

"
I WASN'T AN ART DIRECTOR
AT *VOGUE* FOR NOTHING!
"

THE HUNTING LODGE

Things Nicky Haslam
Finds 'Common'

Scented candles
Film stars
Celebrity chefs
Ibiza
Bottled water
Living statues
Polo
Not eating carbs
Confidence

Richard
Skiing
Airline
Saying 'bye bye'
Oxfordshire
Expensive bikes
Jazz
Halloween
Organic food

© Juergen Teller

Loving your parents
Personal trainers
Jet lag
Being ill
Glass fruit in a bowl
Relaxing
iPods and box sets
Cappuccinos after 11am
Pronouncing the 'e' in 'furore'
Coloured bath towels
Vodka tonic

Caribbean at Christmas
Most young Royals
Dress codes
Cufflinks and shirt studs
Scottish accents
Speeches at weddings
James Bond
Gourmet canapés
Using dog walkers
Going to the gym
Minding about smoking

Cecil Beaton, David Bailey, and Richard Avedon were creative collaborators of his while at *Vogue* and *Harper's Bazaar*. And working under the editorship of the legendary and much-admired style icon Diana Vreeland, Nicky, having started at *Vogue* before her, remembers excited titters going round his department in 1962, when news blew in that she'd be leaving the then more popular *Harper's Bazaar* to join them.

His musical hero Cole Porter, whose songs Nicky started performing at London cabaret nights in 2009, became a friend in Porter's later years. One night, at his apartment in the Waldorf Towers in New York, he offered his frail fingers for a brief serenade at the piano—a moment Nicky treasures.

In one excerpt in his memoir he remembers the "white-gloved hand" of Jackie Kennedy ushering him and pal Jane Ormsby-Gore over at Le Club on East 55th Street. Due to board the Greyhound bus in a few hours, to Washington's British embassy where Jane's parents lived, the story went that Jane was embarrassed to go over and let slip they were too broke to afford a more glamorous mode of travel. After the fourteen-hour bus journey they were greeted at the embassy with a message from "Jackie," wondering why "on earth" they had not come with her on the presidential train.

Francis Bacon and Lucian Freud came to regular dinner parties thrown by Nicky's lover, artist Michael Wishart, before they all headed for a night out at London's Colony Club together. Remaining friends with Freud, when Nicky went into hospital for cancer treatment half a century later, he received an ink-smudged and unpunctuated postcard with "See you soon enjoy the MORPHINE Love Lucian" penned on it.

One of the wildest tales is of dining at Park Lane night club the Saddle Room, and witnessing Mick Jagger, a young LSE student, expose himself to American film star Anthony Steele and his wife, seated at the next table. They had apparently been commenting loudly for some time about how androgynous he looked. Fed up, Jagger went over to their table and unzipped his trousers. Presumably no further confusion ensued.

Nicky is blessed with the most vivid memory for names, faces, places, and anecdotes but I wonder are there any events that top the lot? "The party after Prince Charles's wedding given by the Queen at Claridge's," Nicky replies.

"It started at 5pm and when you walked in there was every crowned head … and Princess Grace and Mrs. Reagan were looking at themselves on the television. There was this feeling of being with all these artists, Freddie Ashton—that sort of world … We ate delicious breakfast food, and they flew Lester Lanin, the great band leader, over from New York. I remember the Queen and Prince Philip starting the dancing, which was wonderful. They danced all night with each other and in and out of people and you could practically say 'Oi—my turn!' There was no formality at all."

With the vibrant and well-travelled life Nicky created for himself, it is difficult not to think of the years of entrapment he experienced as a young boy with polio, and the story of his beloved maid-cum-nanny Teresa ushering the fragile ten-year-old in his pyjamas away from an open window at Great Hundridge Manor, the Buckinghamshire house where he grew up. "I was in a shell for nine months," he says, referring to the plaster casts on his legs.

PREVIOUS SPREAD
Spot a match box sent by Beata Heuman, the Luke Edward Hall drawing disguising the motion sensor beneath Nicky's painted cherry tree branches; a cardboard box painted to look like a Chinese vase; the Hunting Lodge's visitors' book; a pineapple ice-bucket; a portrait of Lucian Freud bought from the railings at Green Park; Nicky's new Doc Martens lace-up shoes; and a photograph of Prince and Princess Michael of Kent they sent him.

OPPOSITE
Nicky's bedroom with Mauny bamboo wallpaper applied to the canopy bed headboard and footer and photographer's reflector fabric used to line his bed hanging.

It was in this attic room that his mother's friends would visit. "Everyone would come up. I was like a circus attraction." Putting on the wind-up gramophone, they would roll up the carpet to foxtrot round his bed. "It was wonderful. That's how I learnt all the Cole Porter songs."

Although he was encouraged to interreact with his parents' friends, among them the writer H. G. Wells, Nicky's mother, Diamond Louise Constance (née Ponsonby), goddaughter to Queen Victoria, rarely went up to his bedroom. His father, diplomat William Heywood Haslam, not often home from London till he had gone to sleep, would occasionally come up to say goodnight.

Teresa cared for him daily and slept by his side when he was most vulnerable from illness. When I ask him to tell me more about her, he says a little tearfully: "Oh, I can't. Read about her in my book . . ."

It certainly brings poignancy to the offence of "loving one's parents" cited in Nicky's popular tongue-in-cheek *Evening Standard* column "How Common!" Yet it was not un-common for children of upper-class families of his generation to have closer relationships with a maid or nanny, their parents' affection being surplus to requirements when someone was employed to do it for them. (These days, it's somewhat frowned upon not to give your child a hug, at least once.)

With two years spent in one room, albeit within the walls of the William and Mary manor house remodelled by architect Clough Williams-Ellis, reading, listening to music, arranging doll's house furniture, and gazing out of the window, perhaps over the Cecil Pinsent-designed garden, but unable to interact with other children and with his two brothers and half-sister away at school, I wonder how much of this experience shaped Nicky's outlook on life, his zest to be out and about and meet people. I am also curious about what such drawn-out restriction did to a young boy's imagination, creativity, and perceptiveness.

His room at Eton was, perhaps, our first glimpse. He says: "My tutor used to bring his dinner guests round to see it—like a cabaret. It had fake grass on the floor and a huge lit-up photograph of James Dean from Rebel Without a Cause. Everyone had flying ducks by Peter Scott and horrible cretonne curtains. I had an ermine I'd bought at a theatrical shop and a pelmet I'd made from thick, white ostrich feathers."

He excelled in art at school, but feeling more akin with the older generation, on leaving he attracted a circle of actors, artists, set designers, photographers, and filmmakers—Lady Diana Cooper, David Bailey, Oliver Messel, and Cecil Beaton among them. He found their company hugely inspiring, as he did the places to which these friendships took him.

He moved to Pimlico, attended an art course, then worked for British *Vogue* before heading across the pond. A career in the art department at American *Vogue* proved promising, but was cut shorter than his editor had hoped after he fell in love with American banking heir James Davison and bought a ranch in Arizona 2,000 miles away to breed horses. In awe of this move, I ask whether he went all out on the cowboy front. He describes his blue jeans, cowboy boots, and leather chaps that local native American women would soften for wear by chewing. "I mean, who *doesn't* want to be a cowboy?! It was the least I could do on a ranch," Nicky says. The very least.

FOLLOWING SPREAD
Cocktail hour in lederhosen. The engraving above Nicky's head, MMXIII FECIT, translates to Made in 2013, which was when the folly was built. In the same year it won the Georgian Group's Giles Worsley Award for a New Building in a Georgian Context.

PAGES 124–25
View past the indoor cherry blossom into Nicky's sitting room, with blinds made up in NH Design Shutter Stripe fabric. Watercolours from projects past are mounted on the wall and a selection of Pevsner Buildings of England *reference books sit on a tiered stand, among others on fashion and interiors, including some of Nicky's own.*

Six years later, the relationship ended, and his proverbial boots were hung up. On returning to England in 1972 he started up as an interior designer. His first commission was a townhouse for Alexander Hesketh. The English peer was one of many ranch visitors who had fallen in love with the couple's Western style and Native American decor.

In the early 1980s Nicky opened a Pimlico Road showroom with partner Paolo Moschino before they went their own ways in 1995, leaving the name "Nicholas Haslam" with Moschino and beginning again on his own. The NH Design studio was born and through it a host of talent has traversed, including Cath Kidston and Beata Heuman. Its winning aesthetic combines a bountiful knowledge and appreciation for architecture, exposure to the theatre, and love of set design, but above all Nicky's wit, charm, and penchant for the unexpected.

Secret doors revealing rooms accessed through busy wallpaper, a painted skylight depicting the faux night sky above a bed with a star sign mapped out in Swarovski crystals, a fluted half column ascending a dining-room wall only to appear broken before reaching the ceiling—his so-called "sham ruin": it is no surprise that requests from around the world came flooding. No request was too extravagant. "I once had to design a pole-dancing roof terrace. I added huge classical fibreglass statues of the four seasons to disguise the poles from the neighbours," Nicky remembers.

He produced a Gothic-inspired furniture collection for OKA and co-designed an ever-popular fabric collection, Random Harvest, with Canadian colleague Colette van den Thillart.

One dream project was his beloved Hunting Lodge at Odilham in Hampshire, formerly owned by English interior design legend John Fowler, which Nicky rented from the National Trust in 1978. Restoring and decorating the striking Jacobean-fronted hidden jewel, Nicky, needle in hand, even tapestried a stool with the pattern of the lodge's window trellis and a border inspired by its Gothic gables.

Unable to renew the lease in 2017, Nicky sold almost forty years of contents through Bonham's auction house: a popular sale albeit, like many of its ilk, a rather sad one.

Visiting Nicky in his newly decorated cross-shaped pavilion, near the gates of the Daylesford Estate in Gloucestershire—old oaks and limes on one side and more recently planted copper beech copse on the other—the view from his sitting room over open parkland is serene. This was a gift from a friend for his lifetime, on the one condition—that he decorate it.

The first thing I note is the beautiful modern art sculptures atop a glass pendant corridor lantern. "Oh, those are cherry tree branches I picked outside and painted white." The bamboo-inlaid wardrobe is exquisite. "Ikea," he replies. "The bamboo is Mauny papier peint I cut out and stuck in the recesses." Surely, *that's* marble is my next thought. "Paint effect," Nicky says telepathically, motioning to the chest of drawers.

Stubbing my toe on a heavy triangular footstool, I notice it clinks. "Oh, you are clever. I'd quite forgotten they were in there!" he says, lifting up the lid to reveal a dozen miniature bottles of Bollinger champagne, unopened.

I am enjoying the spirit of this visit. His talent for creating beauty, kissed by the magic of theatre, is remarkably inspiring. "I could decorate a room in brown paper if you needed me to," he said once.

There is a porcelain trinket box printed with the watercolour of a Christmas card I learn Nicky was commissioned to paint for a friend. It depicts the façade of a Georgian townhouse, painted on pretty bordered art paper, the top sheet's edges curled up in trompe-l'oeil style, to reveal evidence of a discarded draft below. But, only thirteen of the twenty windows are decorated with festive greenery.

"It got so boring doing all those wreaths," he says. There is discernible proof of this fatigue, as the brush itself, still wet with verdant paint, makes an appearance, painted in by the last half-finished garland.

Opening the smooth-hinged china lid reveals little chocolate eggs glinting in shiny foil, an inscription on the underside reads: "Nicky, you are a genius! All love Carole."

And I think Carole has a point.

HENRY 'CHIPS'
CHANNON
THE DIARIES 1918-38

A DOVECOTE HERITAGE

TROY HOUSE

Scout Magic

NICKY HASLAM

FOLLY in GRANDEUR

WOLFGANG-ADAM TÖPFFER

GLOUCESTERSHIRE 1:
THE COTSWOLDS

OXFORDSHIRE

NH

SUSIE LAU

CURIOUSER &
CURIOUSER

THERE MAY BE more pictures of her on city pavements around the globe than tourist snaps of Beatles fans on the Abbey Road zebra crossing. I, for one, would blissfully paper my hypothetically spacious dressing room walls with hundreds of "Susie Bubble" outfits and I am certain there would be no pattern repeat. Her library of looks is endlessly inspiring, irresistibly moreish, and utterly unique.

With a penchant for Molly Goddard's multilayered tulle, Simone Rocha's voluminous frills and embellished shoes that look more like ornaments than footwear, it comes as a surprise that Susie's wardrobe, albeit "walk-in"—as long as you keep it to two steps—is, in fact, tiny.

"My dream would be to have everything breathe, wholly visible as opposed to me having to dig things out." If only. Apart from the inconvenience, she should really have a museum dedicated to her wardrobe, comparable to a modern Marie Antoinette's, with a shoe rack Imelda Marcos would envy: not in quantity, but for its exquisite curation. She does not appear to do "classic wardrobe staples," "an LBD," or "shoes that go with everything." Instead, there is every sort of pleating, quilting, silk, satin, faux fur, tulle, mesh, tassel, metallic, and printed fabric in every imaginable shade.

Spilling from the shelves I note black and red Prada shoes with flames shooting out from the heel, furry metallic Salvatore Ferragamo boots, slouched green silk knee-highs with embroidered dragons climbing up them and a pair of red check bouclé Gucci slippers parked under her bed. A peek into her accessories drawers reveals a floral beaded eyepatch; a pair of golden metallic ears that clip on like earrings; tights—rose print on one leg, metallic green on the other; and a tiny palm-sized jacket-shaped patent leather bag on a miniature coat hanger in a pint-sized clothing bag.

Her six-year-old daughter Nico's room has all the things you might expect a little girl to have: a Hello Kitty rabbit night light, miniature doll's house, Little Miss books, and a pink paisley fabric rocking horse, as well as pieces that look like tiny versions of mummy's clothes.

Pastel blue and pink marbled paper packing boxes from fashion boutique Matches and an old Globe-Trotter-style suitcase appliquéd with flowers fill the gap under the sofa. Susie confesses to being a hoarder and admits to buying things that have no real use other than she "just likes the pattern," but says she is fussy about the things that come into her wardrobe: "I'm a research fiend. I like to dig a little bit deeper. I like context and specificity. I'm a very curious person probably to the point of being a bit annoying."

Drawn to "super interesting design details" and "clothes that tell a story," her travels also add magic to her finds. "I have been to so many places, working in fashion and always think of it as being much broader than just the four capitals," she says, referring to London, Milan, New York and Paris. Trips to Shanghai and Lagos have widened her perception of how experimental people are. This explains many of the labels in her wardrobe that I have never heard of. "I feel so privileged when I look at my wardrobe. It's a documentation of my life," she says.

The pleasure she gets from many of her clothes is often accompanied by the memories they bring back. "Even this old tie-dye," she says, pulling at her T-shirt, "reminds me of rummaging shopping trips in Japan ... to find second-hand Comme [des Garçons] or Junya [Watanabe]." She treasures a dress from

PAGE 126
Lunch on the counter in vintage Comme des Garçons, with something delicious stewing in a pot for her daughter's week ahead. Susie has an enticing array of cookbooks and some Assassin Puffs cereal sent to her as Killing Eve *promotional material.*

ABOVE
A mooncake jade bunny made at Susie's Dot Dot bubble tea and waffle restaurant in Stoke Newington.

OPPOSITE
Susie's daughter's bedroom, the ultimate little girl's room, with every shade of pastel pink; Minna Parikka plimsolls with bunny ears; a dinosaur duvet; Shrimps cushion; and books on Maya Angelou and Coco Chanel. A Chinese New Year outfit sent from Hong Kong hangs in the centre.

> EVERY SINGLE THING I OWN
> HAS A STORY AND AN EMOTION
> ATTACHED TO IT.

Mary Katrantzou's graduate collection and a piece she was given by Yves Saint Laurent designer Anthony Vaccarello "back when he was doing his little label, we were hanging out in his apartment, and he wasn't anywhere near as starry as he is now."

I am interested in her buying habits, because most fashion people can put a great look together but Susie's originality and choice, even with pieces fresh off the catwalk, make her stand out from the crowd. "Eclectic," "addictive," and "unapologetically fun" are some of the terms I have heard to describe her style, but her reputation as "queen of street style" does not do her justice. Using herself as a canvas—with her trademark glossy black hair and 1960s sloping fringe framing her pretty face—her layering of pattern, colour and shape, and her era-mixing and fabric combinations, are truly works of art.

"As a life skill, that's maybe not super useful," she says, self-deprecatingly.

On the contrary, this futile skill has earned her half a million social media followers, and a career as a fashion journalist and consultant, whose opinion is valued enough for her to be flown round the world. Like many creatives, she finds it difficult to pinpoint the process, but nonetheless I ask her to analyse how she puts a look together: "I'm a very visual person. I gravitate towards different patterns and colours. It's not random. But it's not mathematical. It's more like, well this shade will go well with this."

I think there is another reason.

My own mother always said about style, "You either have it or you don't." It all sounded a bit mystical to me. But, as with many mothers' words that finally ring true, it is often our experience that brings them to the fore. During my styling career, dressing people with extraordinary style as well as those who find the art of attire more perplexing, I've learnt that, with practice, a mentor or methods set in place, you can improve the skill, but in the same way some are good with words and bad at numbers, others are good or bad with shape and colours—a sort of sartorial dyslexia you might call it—and although, like anything, you can get better with practice, for someone to really shine, I believe there is indeed an innate ability or "eye" present from the start.

At university, feeling shy and unconfident, Susie instinctively nurtured this "eye," and used it to find her voice—taking pictures of her outfits in her bedroom mirror, and writing a blog—sowing the seed for her journalism career. She says: "It felt so easy to put together a cool, crazy outfit as opposed to say . . . going up to someone and asking them out . . . which I've never actually done."

Previously, during the 1990s, Susie attended the all-girls Henrietta Barnett School, a London grammar in Hampstead, London. She says: "I wasn't the smartest person in a school of very smart people." To boot, academia was set on a pedestal and fashion generally regarded with contempt. "People were very anti-fashion actually. There was a group of pupils that campaigned against skirts because they thought it was a feminist slur," she remembers, looking bemused.

A little further down the hill, Susie's Camden life comprised a multitude of ethnicities, cultures, and tribes. Neo-punks and goths in tulle and leather walked in and out of her parents' takeaway restaurant, art students and musicians headed to live music hotspots, while tourists arriving on canal boats made

PAGES 130-131
Susie's sitting room is full of fashion tomes and decorative packaging. Marbleised Matches Fashion boxes are stowed above her writing desk. There are old and Instamatic cameras dotted around surfaces and a circular framed photograph of Susie as a baby in her mother's arms.

PREVIOUS SPREAD
A bag stand to match Susie's overflowing wardrobe; a wonderful old Covent Garden storage trolley she uses for cookbooks and spices; delicious slices of matcha crêpe cake from Dot Dot; Gucci ear-cuffs; and a surreal pen and ink artwork, drawn by her sister, hanging in her bathroom.

OPPOSITE
Blowing bubbles in a vintage kimono and Maison Margiela mules in front of a backdrop of hats used as wall hangings.

ABOVE
A six-inch-tall miniature leather coat handbag, which came with its own tiny transparent clothing cover and hanger.

beelines for steaming gumbo, paella, and jerk chicken in the open-air food markets. Through narrow allies of buttered sweetcorn vans, fashion designers and vintage scavengers, looking for inspiration, braved the rabbit warren of stalls in the historic Camden market stables, burlesque dancers sized up corsets along the wharf, and Madame Jojo's drag queens swept the high street's "alternative" shoe stores for the perfect size twelve platform boots. Considering the eclectic spirit of Susie's borough, it seemed surprising that her school friends were outraged by skirts.

At home, Susie observed her hardworking parents running the takeaway restaurant on Parkway. Though her mother dressed primarily for the practicalities of restaurant life, Susie says, laughing, that she is more than willing to point out an unflattering outfit or picture of her. "I come from a humble working-class family and my parents are not very 'fashion people.' My mum's interest in fashion disappeared in her twenties when she had kids." Imitating her mother's voice, Susie says: "As soon as I lost my waist, I lost interest!" A glimpse of this phase was passed down in the form of some "slouchy leather 1980s boots" and a "Burberry trench coat" her mother had found in a charity shop.

Having emigrated from Hong Kong in the 1970s, her parents made their children—Susie and her three sisters, Louisa, Yonnika, and Jennifer—aware of how it was to set up a new life in another country and work hard to bring them up. "It's ingrained in us," Susie says, feeling her generation had an easier time. "Multiculturalism—maybe I know a very idealised version of it, because in my eyes I never saw any friction in London. I have experienced microaggressions, but I could count them on my hands."

The family watched English period dramas like *The House of Eliott* and her parents held similarly traditional views about their daughters' upbringing. "It's a bit like Chinese *Pride and Prejudice,* because none of us are married. Well, I have a daughter but then I'm separated from her dad. So, my mum is like, 'I despair!,'" she says, laughing and putting a hand to her forehead in a mock period drama swoon. But she suspects she may have slipped through the net of approval having given them a much-loved granddaughter.

Back in Hong Kong, it was customary to dress Chinese children up, so she and her eldest sister Louisa, often mistaken for twins, were dressed in "matchy-matchy red velvet dresses" and "dalmatian print coats" sent over in care packages from friends and family in China. Susie still has a few little "red satin waistcoats" for Nico, whose arrival prompted a newfound pride in her "Chinese side," the importance of traditions and teaching her daughter about them.

They seem a close family, often meeting up for celebratory occasions to cook Chinese banquets. Food is evidently deeply ingrained in her heart. She opened Dot Dot, a London bubble tea and waffle restaurant in 2021; manages to base outfits around "treating herself to a dozen oysters;" finds hand-making noodles therapeutic; and creates the most wonderful Japanese cartoon character cakes for her daughter.

She is a natural in the kitchen, and I am as mesmerised by pictures of her food as I am by the looks that accompany them. Whether it is puffed sleeves and bao buns, mermaid cake and pastels, Fendi pasta with Fendi shoes, or bubble tea and polka dots, this sensual vibrance is all part of what makes Susie so deliciously appealing.

CHARLIE CASELY-HAYFORD

REBEL WITH
A CAUSE

THOSE IMPOSING steel-toed twelve-hole ex-army boots and red socks exposed by beautifully tailored cropped trousers have been a source of ocular appreciation for me for many years: footwear that might intimidate if it were not for the feet of the polite and friendly giant inhabiting them. Charlie Casely-Hayford's upper body is often distinguished by a boxy Crombie-style jacket, broken up with slices of monochrome, either blocked dramatically across the front or in the more subtle form of a white linen sliver just visible above his perfectly angled pocket, offset by pops of colour at the ankle or the glimpse of a T-shirt print. Each detail breaks up yet accentuates the space left on his six-foot four-inch frame, with his asymmetrically twisted Afro adding a few more centimetres besides.

There is something classic yet unorthodox about this look, sharp yet roughed up, nostalgic yet modern, street, intelligent, formal, and rebellious all at once. From a traditional men's tailoring point of view, things are not quite how they ought to be; from an aesthetics perspective, they are spot on. Simply put, Charlie looks achingly good in his clothes. But most satisfyingly, this beautifully put-together look, coined at one point by *Dazed* magazine as "Sartorial Skinhead," is unmistakably his own.

Sometimes, being given the opportunity to make sense of something you have admired from afar can take away some of the magic, but in this case it only adds to it.

Charlie's look is inspired by the original 1960s British skinhead culture that preceded punks: a subculture of working-class youngsters with shaved heads, cut-off jeans, and work boots, often steel-toed or Doc Martens. The look was embraced in solidarity for those who felt socially alienated, rejecting the establishment and conservatism of the 1950s and 1960s. Elements of mod, British Jamaican and Jamaican immigrant rude boy subculture were adopted by the skinheads as there was much overlap between these groups in poorer British neighbourhoods and in turn were heavily influenced by reggae, dub, ska, African-American soul, rhythm and blues, and funk music. "My white pocket square is a nod to the establishment—I like the contrast between the two worlds in one look," Charlie says.

It takes most people well into their thirties to work out what suits them, but as far as I remember, I have always associated this strong image with Charlie, ever since I met him when we were kicking about town in our early twenties. Is it possible to have always looked this cool? "Surely," I ask, "you must have gone through some questionable wardrobe phases?"

"In answer to that I would have to say not really," comes the earnest reply, said without a hint of arrogance. "I grew up with parents in the fashion industry so I didn't really have a choice." Even as a small child he remembers he and his sister Alice being dressed to the nines in "statement coats, berets—the works!." Living with his parents until he was twenty, he would leave their Hackney house to go out partying and "every night they would essentially assess my outfits," he describes.

This image is golden. While most British parents bumping into their teenagers trying to creep out the door before being seen would be asking inane questions like "What *are* you wearing?!" and "Is that

PAGE 140
Charlie, in a chestnut brown glen check Casely-Hayford suit, sat in the bespoke tailoring suite in front of photographs of twentieth-century artists. He and his wife, the interior designer Sophie Ashby, both studied history of art—at the Courtauld and Leeds, respectively.

OPPOSITE
The Casely-Hayford storefront, a stone's throw from the Firehouse on Chiltern Street, London.

FOLLOWING SPREAD
Perched on Charlie's hand is the first pair of boots his father made for him when the elder Casely-Hayford was in design college. An African Victorian Feminist is a book about Charlie's grandfather's second wife. The gilt frame houses a collage of the original Joe Casely-Hayford clothing labels, and there is an ode to a three-year-old Charlie by his dad Joe, interviewed in a press article, below.

AN AFRICAN
VICTORIAN FEMINIST

The Life and Times of
Adelaide Smith Casely Hayford
1868-1960

A personal chronicle of
social change in West Africa,
incorporating her memoirs

ADELAIDE M. CROMWELL

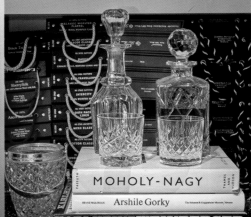

MOHOLY-NAGY

Arshile Gorky

KARLHEINZ WEINBERGER

18 JUNE 1989

SUNDAY
EXPRESS
magazine

Joe Casely-Hayford, fashion
designer, is one of our brightest
style stars. The darling of
popstars such as Annie Lennox,
his three-year-old son Charlie is
still his greatest fan.

"We share the same
birthday — he was my
best ever birthday
present. He's wonderful,
almost a perfect child.
He's all those clichés
doting fathers spout
when they talk about
their children. He's the
source of immense
pleasure and great fun.
He's kind and gentle and
caring. Being a father
changed my lifestyle and
my priorities. It made me
realise that there is real
life beyond the catwalk.
I used to be a real
fashionaholic, but you
can't pose with two
children. I'm 33 now
and still have to remind
myself that I'm an adult.
Charlie and I are on the
same wavelength. I'm
a father but it doesn't
mean I have to grow
up. I'm still just a big
boy really.

JOE Prince of Wales check
double-breasted jacket, £290,
matching trousers, £150; silk
sailor collar shirt, £132; all by
Joe Casely-Hayford, from
Jones (01-240 8312). Leather
slip-ons, £195, from New and
Lingwood (01-493 9621).
CHARLIE Baggy hand-
knitted sweater, £90, by
Norma Greenwood for Joe
Casely-Hayford; checked
Bermudas, £85, by Joe Casely-
Hayford, both to order (01-437
9696). T-shirt, Charlie's own.
Stripped socks £1.99, from Sock
Shop. Two-tone blue Mary
Janes, £48, from Buckle My
Shoe (01-935 5589). Conical
hat from a selection at John
Lewis (01-629 7711).
Grooming by Ruby Hammer.

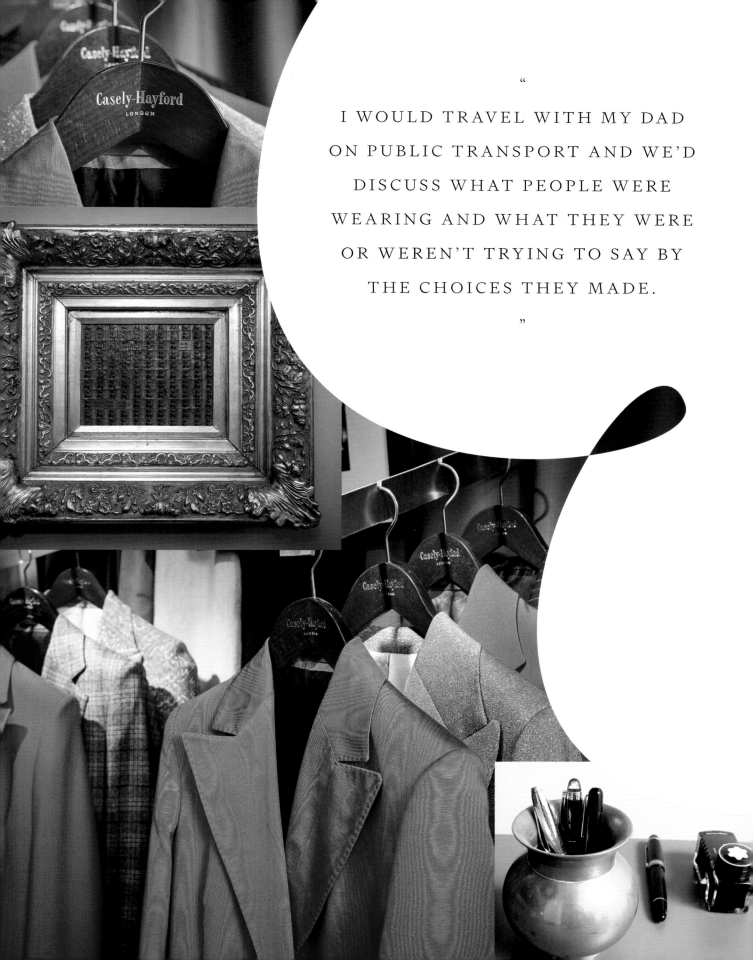

"

I WOULD TRAVEL WITH MY DAD
ON PUBLIC TRANSPORT AND WE'D
DISCUSS WHAT PEOPLE WERE
WEARING AND WHAT THEY WERE
OR WEREN'T TRYING TO SAY BY
THE CHOICES THEY MADE.

"

a skirt or a belt?" and gaining little popularity in the process, Charlie's pre-night-out panel was made up of husband-and-wife fashion duo Maria and Joe Casely-Hayford, two top Central Saint Martins fashion design graduates who had been industry partners since 1980, the year they married. The Joe Casely-Hayford brand had been nominated for designer-of-the-year awards before Charlie was born. Joe had designed for Vivienne Westwood and Joseph; styled pages for *The Face*, *i-D*, and the FT's *How to Spend It*; and in 1992, when Charlie was six, had a suit worn by U2's Bono, the first man ever shot for a British *Vogue* cover. When Charlie was nineteen, his dad was creative director of Gieves & Hawkes.

While going through the somewhat gruelling experience every teenager has of working out who they are, what shape their body is taking on, and what works sartorially by experimenting and making regrettable mistakes in the process, Charlie had two of the best and most inspiring teachers to guide him.

"I became very conscious of what worked, what didn't, and why. I learnt to dissect clothing in a kind of mathematical way because I would quite often travel with my dad on public transport and we'd discuss what people were wearing and what they were or weren't trying to say by the choices they made. So I began thinking like that from a very young age."

Helping shape this aesthetic was an upbringing and education that included his parents' Dalston factory, somewhere he would hang out after school, and his home in Hackney, which during the 1990s was a multicultural melting pot. Here, at the bustling Ridley Road Market—a place where fruit, vegetables, clothing, and fabric were sold—he would observe Nigerians in their Sunday dress, Hasidic Jews from Stanford Hill, and a big Irish community congregating and going about their business. "It was really vibrant, bright, colourful … a lot going on," he says.

His education spanned an impressive array of traditional British institutions: the Barbican's arty Charterhouse Square School and then the academic Westminster School—both former sixteenth-century monasteries in central London—followed by the renowned public school Harrow, founded under a Royal Charter granted by Queen Elizabeth I and where Winston Churchill had been a pupil. Charlie said that no one had heard of Dalston and Hackney when he arrived at Harrow, but by the time he left they were becoming trendy areas and people were moving there.

Although an academic pupil who enjoyed and appreciated his schooling, he also describes Harrow, in particular, as having "kind of stringent uniforms …and you could only show your individualism in the smallest way." Sunday dress included a tailcoat, waistcoat, and morning trousers and on weekdays a straw boater was an optional accessory. "So, there were these two disparate worlds colliding and shaping my mindset, which was quite interesting."

I wondered whether being taught to work out what he wanted to say through the prism of clothes not only kept him from herd-following, but also accelerated the process of figuring himself out much earlier than most. Actually, he feels that, as his parents were so clued up about everything, it was "sometimes hard to experience things for myself." It was only when he got to Central Saint Martins, where everyone was

OPPOSITE
Charlie's desk with a cow horn clothes brush and shoehorn, Trudon Ottoman candle, and Mont Blanc stationery, with one pen engraved with his name and another inscribed, intriguingly, "Mr Daim."

FOLLOWING SPREAD
The shop interior, filled with art books and African art, designed by Charlie's wife, Sophie. The photograph behind the desk is by Lakin Ogunbanwo.

ALICE TEMPERLEY

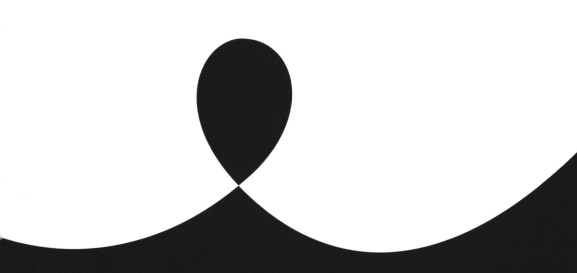

WELCOME TO
WONDERLAND

would model for her childrenswear collection. "She had a house full of arts, crafts, and fabric," Alice remembers.

At the "little farmhouse" there was no television until Alice was eleven, and even then, the children were not allowed to watch it until dark, having to make do with other things to entertain themselves during daylight hours. Perhaps it is unsurprising all four entered creative fields: Henry as a film-maker, Matilda as a photographer (and also working to take over the cider farm), and Mary with her own skincare range.

The TV's arrival for Alice was a poignant one, prompting a lifelong addiction to black-and-white movies. Obsessed with film stars like Ginger Rogers and Marlene Dietrich and the clothes of American costumier Edith Head, Alice gorged on these films when her parents thought she had gone to bed. "I hadn't seen anything quite like it as far as the way people dressed, listened to music, wore jewellery, and had their hair done. It was literally like a drug I was on all the time." Transporting her from farm life to another world of music, romance, and decadence, instead of a post-trip hangover, she was left with a brilliant imprint on which to draw for inspiration.

The strong female characters she encountered in this world of theatrical glamour, resonated. "They weren't just movie stars but proper characters," she explains. They were not necessarily conventionally beautiful or classically styled but "they had their own voice, their own thing going on." As well as Dietrich, Alice's style inspirations include Amelia Earheart, Carine Roitfeld, and Diana Vreeland, each clearly defined by a distinctive voice and unconventionality.

"It's like designing collections. You shouldn't be trying to keep everyone happy … You should be listening to that one voice."

For Alice, finding her own voice, did not happen immediately. Through her teens, she morphed out of dungarees and into Doc Martens and ripped jeans, listened to reggae, and even in her school uniform managed to look so scruffy that the headmaster refused to make her a prefect until her father complained about discrimination.

After school she studied design at Central Saint Martins before going on to the Royal College of Art for a Master's in textiles. She started her business in 2000 with her then-boyfriend Lars von Bennigsen, sister Mary, and friend Sophie Cranston.

She married Lars in 2002, giving birth to her son Fox six years later (five days after a Spring/Summer show). When I first met Alice in 2011, the year the Queen pinned an MBE to her suit jacket, little Fox was very much a feature of her work life, tottering about happily at early evening fashion events, occasionally stopping nonchalantly to talk to a supermodel or pull at his mother's sleeve for attention. Despite the many famous fans of the Temperley brand, including Arizona Muse, Jacquetta Wheeler, Beyoncé, the Duchess of Cambridge and Gillian Anderson, it did not take me long to clock Alice's siblings and parents among the London glitterati. The support is reciprocal,

OPPOSITE
Alice on her landing, underneath the Titian-esque ceiling mural painted on the underside of the cupola. She is wearing a Temperley dress to match the moody sky overhead.

FOLLOWING SPREAD
Snuggled up with her son, Fox, Alice luxuriates in her grand bed—twice the width of a standard double—furnished with a leopard print spread from the Temperley home collection and set into the curved wall of her bedroom.

PAGES 168–69
Indian dolls hang outside Alice's bedroom and no mirror ball bubble bath is complete without a hat and bottle of Burrow Hill cider from Alice's parents' farm. There is superb storage at Cricket Court for fabric cuttings and samples, apothecary needs, a plinth for the resident taxidermy puffer fish, and the humorous glass lamp on the sill of Alice's wood-panelled office for, ahem … sugar?

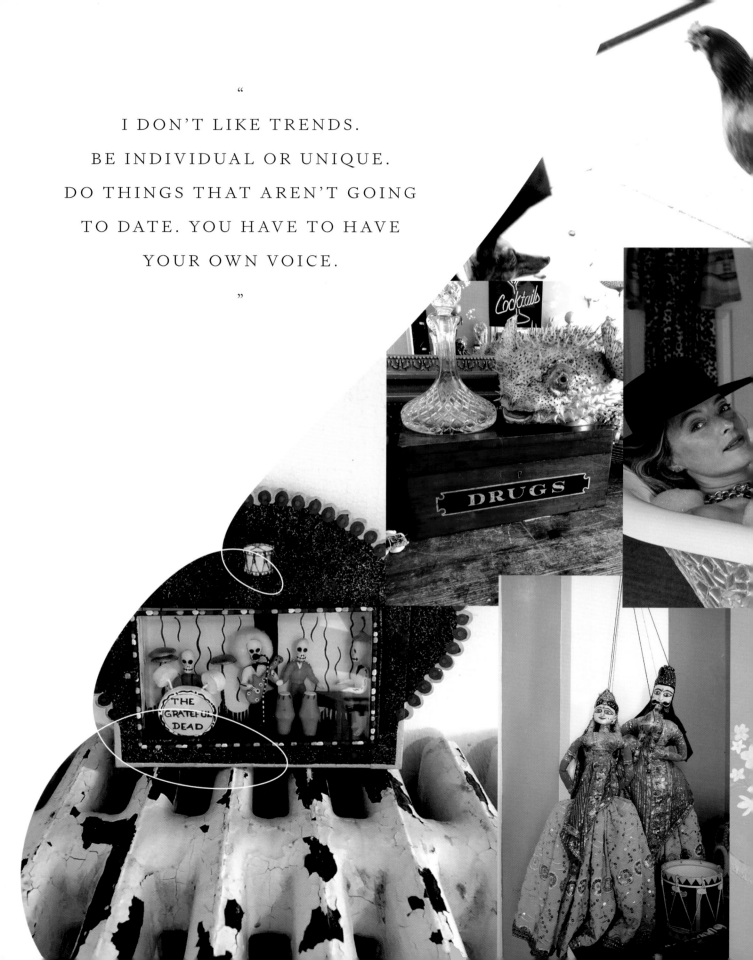

"
I DON'T LIKE TRENDS.
BE INDIVIDUAL OR UNIQUE.
DO THINGS THAT AREN'T GOING
TO DATE. YOU HAVE TO HAVE
YOUR OWN VOICE.
"

too, whether it is turning up *en famille* for an exhibition of Matilda's, or doling out cider from their van at Glastonbury.

As I wonder if Fox is showing any sartorial sense yet, Alice tells me the story of a shopping trip to Bicester Village where, she explains, he can go off on his own and choose "one item." He selects "a gold and white leather bomber jacket with sequins." "It was quite funny; he was nine," smiles Alice.

With sister Mary and her four children close by, and Cricket Court used for fashion campaigns and Alice's annual summer birthday party, the house is often filled with familiar faces, just the way she likes it. Alice is at her happiest "at home in the countryside, just enjoying the simple, wholesome, good things, like beautiful, long evenings with laughter and friends."

It is in Somerset, where she only recently returned, that Alice's voice is most strong. Whether dressed in a workman's cap, waistcoat and braces in the textile room, or dancing barefoot in a ballgown in the bear pit, she is home.

PREVIOUS SPREAD
Alpaca feeding time in the meadow at the south front of the house, which has traditional English pebble dash around the ground floor level. The remains of a Tudor bear pit, just visible under the lower terrace, are turned into a dance floor during summer parties. Bear pits, or bear gardens, were fashionable additions to grand gardens during the sixteenth, seventeenth, and eighteenth centuries, when the gruesome entertainment of bear-baiting was popular in Britain. The spectacle was banned in the nineteenth century.

OPPOSITE
The corner of the piano room has a safari theme, with a zebra rocking horse and an old hippo skull on the table with a pith helmet perched on top.

BELOW
Alice's fabric scissors.

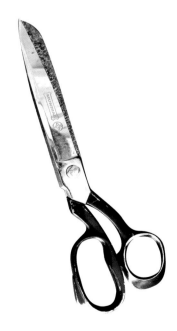

ALICE TEMPERLEY

PHILIP COLBERT

HOW DO YOU LIKE
YOUR EGGS?

VENESSA
BELL
IS AN
IDIOT

him the name Lobster Man in South Korea and Mr. Lobsterrr in Russia, and led the late *Vogue* editor André Leon Talley to describe him as the "godson of Andy Warhol." Philip became fascinated by the relationship each culture had with his brick-pincered sea creature. For some, it represented strength or protection. For others, provoked by seafaring folk tales of lobsters piling 60 centimetres high on beaches, it symbolised abundance. Lobsters have been depicted in mosaics, paintings, on pottery and sculpture since the first century AD. Like humans, they can be left- or right-clawed, but perhaps for Philip the animal simply represents someone finally coming out of their shell.

Although publicly his suits served the purpose of reflecting an alter ego, he found wearing bright colours in the studio affected his clarity of thought, so he adopted all black during winter and, for a short time, all white in summer. "Although white has a lighter vibe, it's not practical because once you're covered in paint, you're no longer white." Still claiming he has no style—just a code to which he sticks—he insists: "I'm not a good dresser. I've found a formula that gets me through the day." In retrospect, he forgives himself for his adolescent grunge period, when he was obsessed with Kurt Cobain, and is more critical of the time when he tried to blend in and express no individuality at all.

When he married Charlotte Boulay-Goldsmith in 2013 he wore a black three-piece suit with

OPPOSITE
The artwork painted on the wooden chest is by Alberto Morrocco and above it hangs an untitled photograph by Charlotte.

ABOVE
Philip in a fried egg suit of his own design in front of an artwork of more sequinned eggs, also by him. He sits on piles of unopened post, the opening of which, he professes, is one of the most boring things in the world.

PHILIP COLBERT

BELOW
*Tea for one and a Rodnik
shark iPhone case.*

OPPOSITE
*The couple's other sitting
room has a Peter Saul
painting above the fireplace,
a Keith Haring baby rocker,
a pushchair designed by
Philip Colbert for Maclaren,
and a watermelon stool they
bought from the Saatchi
Gallery gift shop with a
Charlotte Colbert ceramic
on top.*

his favourite crustacean printed on it, and Charlotte wore a white 1950s-shaped dress she had made herself, inspired by Giorgio de Chirico's Ballets Russes costumes. But this was one of the lobster's last hurrahs in Philip's wardrobe—not so for the golden fallopian tubes necklace made by his wife, a fellow artist, which Philip treasures and never removes. I wonder what she thinks of his printed suits now. He says: "They're like Marmite to Charlotte. She loves the spirit of them but loathes them simultaneously."

Having dreamt of crossing a multitude of creative mediums, Philip has collaborated with interior design companies, children's publishers, confectionary labels, cartoon and comic characters and more recently sportswear brands—a theme he has used in his work extensively: "I love how people of all cultures, classes, and backgrounds can relate to sportswear." In 2020 he launched an exhibition at the Saatchi Gallery only viewable remotely by robot. Each robot travelled on wheels around the gallery with a face resembling a mobile phone screen, filming the exhibition for the live ticket holder displayed on it. Philip, the only human physically present at his exhibition, with two small children at home, was particularly charmed when he came across a robot screen showing thirty primary school children who had logged in to see the exhibition from their classroom. "They all waved. Then the teacher asked me lots of questions," he says.

As Philip has become more heard, his suits have become quieter. He wears less print and opts instead for one colour, teamed with a colour-popping Rodnik cap if the mood strikes him. His red corduroy three-piece suit made by Matt Whitley, tailor to fellow artists Gavin Turk and the Chapman brothers, he describes as an abstract version of the lobster.

Although Philip still admires vulgarity in paintings, he now appreciates what is more palatable. "People love abstract art because they can just sit with it. It's very easy. It's the same with my suits—I actually have some in brown, faun, and other earthy colours. Some of them remind me of Scottish mountains. There's something quite nice about that too," he says, a ticking time bomb away from tweed jacket and clan kilt territory.

RARE BIRDS, TRUE STYLE

MARTHA SITWELL

UNCONVENTIONAL
KNICKER DRAWER

IT WAS WHILE sifting through Lady Sitwell's unconventional knicker drawer, a giant hatbox with the circular logo of Lock & Co. Hatters, St James's Street, London on the front, that I was convinced I would catch her out.

I was mistaken. Inside, there was neither a flash of grey-white cotton nor an M&S label in sight—only a sea of black La Perla lace, every satin shade of Agent Provocateur pink, and a delicate tangle of antique pastel-toned silk corsets and waspies. Down to her underwear, Martha Sitwell's' dedication to vintage style is impressive, if not absolute.

Having observed Martha for nearly ten years, firstly across the room at London society parties and then across dinner tables at country weekends, I noted that she is not someone you can miss. Her distinctive husky laughter is always heard over a crowded room, even with bad acoustics, and she is rarely seen without a Marlboro Red to hand, painted fingers poised to slide yet another cigarette out before slipping the packet snugly back into whatever exquisite vintage bag is dangling from her wrist that night. But the most distinctive thing about Martha is the fact that she never appears to be wearing anything made since 1959.

By about the fifth time I was met with her red lip, pin curls, and ivory silk shirt knotted at her tiny waist, I have to admit my fascination began to grow into a suspicious lust—one that was giving me the increasing urge to break into her house, throw open her cupboard, and find those saggy grey tracksuit bottoms and mud-caked trainers I knew were in there … somewhere. When I finally got to live that particular dream (bar the breaking and entering part), I was sorely disappointed.

During a winter shooting weekend in North Wales, to which Martha had accompanied her (now ex-) husband as "peg pussy" (an excellent term Martha introduced me to, describing the traditional role of a female in the non-shooting party who keeps someone in the shooting party company by standing by their allocated numbered post or peg), I had the opportunity to get to know her a little better. Moving into the dining room for Friday dinner, I let my eyes follow a thin black seam running up the back of her leg from her gold snakeskin Louboutin's. Promptly after the main course I noticed her twist a cigarette into a little embossed silver holder, while waxing lyrical about the lack of decent side-saddle habits available to the hunting community. It occurred to me then that this was less a look and more a persona—one she seems to inhabit wholeheartedly. But where did this obsession with all things old-fashioned come from?

Martha grew up between Belgravia in London and the idyllic north Norfolk countryside near Holt. Most of her time was spent at Shipdham Place in Norfolk, an "over-stuffed" ten-bedroomed Georgian rectory, which was run by her parents as a "restaurant with rooms." The middle child of three girls to mother Melanie (née Irwin), a once Michelin-starred chef who married father Justin de Blank after starting work at one of his pioneering London delis in 1977, Martha remembers them always looking stylish. Her part Dutch part Scottish-English father was particular about his clothes, sticking to a more traditional gentleman's wardrobe but with a European edge, having spent time in France—"Pa didn't own a pair of jeans. He wore a lot of corduroy, three-piece suits, and seersucker"—while her Irish mother was trendier

"
THE BEST THING IS RED LIPSTICK
WHEN YOU'RE FEELING DOWN.
IT CHANGES EVERYTHING.
"

ANDREW LOGAN

THE JACKDAW

PAGE 202
Andrew at the entrance of
the Andrew Logan Museum
of Sculpture, which he
converted from squash
courts that were no longer
in use, in a lime green
leather Armani coat, bought
for a steal in Palm Springs
during a heatwave.

OPPOSITE
On the staircase of the
museum are mirror portraits
of Andrew's parents and
siblings, and in front is an
over-life-sized sculpture of
his friend Zandra Rhodes,
whom, if nudged, sways
from side to side, her hands
in a meditation pose.

FOLLOWING SPREAD
Stood in a bespoke orange
Indian silk Nehru suit in
front of his beautifully kept
bedroom clothes cupboard
brimming with every shade
imaginable. Glass brooches
hang on the interior of the
cupboard doors. He wears
one every day.

PAGES 208–09
His studio houses a caravan,
rendered in the black-and-
white half-timbered style
you see on traditional Welsh
Victorian cottages. Andrew
wears a violet Indian
silk waistcoat with gold
embroidery and matching
velvet crown.

"HAVE YOU EVER made any personal style errors that you regret?" I ask Andrew. He pauses for two seconds then replies resolutely: "None whatsoever."

At first glance, it seems the health and safety situation in his art studio does not fill him with the same certainty. With Andrew in a high-vis vest, I look around at the multi-drawered filing cabinets brimming with mosaic tiles, above which glass jam jars of glitter are suspended. A picture-covered balcony overhangs draped mannequins and easels propped against a parked camper van, curiously rendered in the black-and-white half-timbered style you see on Welsh Victorian houses. Just above my eyeline, swaying pearls dangle from the nipples of a slender sculpture stretched out like a ship's figurehead on his workbench, a golden egg teetering on her outstretched palms.

As I start to weigh up from which direction the risk of falling objects is most probable, I am relieved to learn that the vest is a recent fashion purchase, matching a pair of fluorescent yellow trousers Andrew had already. "I'm like a jackdaw," he says, "drawn to colour and shiny objects." True to his word, I later discover his bedroom painted in the same radiant sunshine lacquer.

The rural Welsh setting of the Old Court House, at Berriew in Montgomeryshire, where Andrew and his partner, Michael Davis, live, is bewitchingly beautiful. Descending a steep hill past the post office, family butchers and a line of half-timbered cottages, you arrive at a bridge crossing the River Severn. On the bank above the crystal water is a winding garden path leading up to the couple's ground-floor balcony. The art studio and Andrew Logan Museum of Sculpture are a stone's throw away on the street side opposite.

Opening the door from the country lane is like plunging into Lewis Carroll's rabbit hole. As extraordinary items swirl past your eyeline, it takes a moment to realise that your feet are on solid ground, albeit in Andrew's kitchen, facing a stuffed toy zebra and an impressive collection of "teapot art." Artwork covers every available wall and an abundance of natural light streams through the sliding balcony doors. The giant chessboard floor leads the eye to the open-plan study beyond, broken up by the slope of a shocking-pink Bauhaus-esque stair bannister. The floor pops brilliantly against spearmint-blue walls and cabinets, and the kitchen's giant silver fridge and chrome extractor fan look like parts from an alien spaceship. A particular favourite are the irresistibly tactile velvet dining chairs, like electrocuted smarties with cow-print seats in their new plush re-coverings, originally courthouse furniture bought at auction.

As well as the perfume of lilies, there is a warm, sweet scent of cooling raspberry jam. The perpetrator of this aroma, Michael, apologises for his cluttered jam jars. Andrew, meanwhile, has found a box of wigs, one of which he is now wearing while stripping mint leaves from their stalks to make our fresh herbal tea.

Up the cerise stairs, carpeted in red and green Scottish tartan, is a crimson movie theatre with a huge state-of-the-art curved screen and a sofa resembling a pair of giant lips. Forty glass mosaic hearts hang on the wall. "I made one for every year Michael and I have been together," Andrew says. A golden palm tree towers over the sofa and I am amused to see architect Michael's desk on the other side of the room, wondering how much work he achieves there, as it feels more like a nightclub than an office.

"
I CAN'T STAND ALL THOSE
FADED FARROW & BALL
WISHY-WASHY COLOURS.
"

MARINA DURHAM & ROSE CHOLMONDELEY

VOYAGE FROM DEVON

THERE IS A FAINT muffled ticking just audible over the simmering purr and occasional crackle from the fire in the hallway at Wembury. It has been lit in anticipation of the sisters' arrival at their Devonshire childhood home. I put my ear up to the mantelpiece clock only to see reflected in the mirror a porcelain Chinese figure in a neck ruff, perched cross-legged on the side table, and recall in a wave of nostalgia that the sound is coming from its tongue gently flapping up and down as the head nods.

I came here as a child and remember being mesmerised by this ornament, seemingly moving of its own accord, which my parents told me not touch, but it was irresistible not to tap the wagging tongue. In a bedroom upstairs, I picture a strawberry blonde pet hamster peering through a doll's house door. Inside was beautiful wallpaper, miniature curtains, exquisite furniture, and a tiny light bulb that turned on and off—an electrical feat my godmother, Emma, the matriarch of the family, had achieved. Returning some thirty years later, I am staying in this exact room, covered wall-to-wall in butterflies, which I suspect weren't always there. But my thoughts are cut short by the sound of footsteps and small voices at the door.

The Countess of Durham and the Marchioness of Cholmondeley, otherwise known as Marina & Rose, their husbands, and seven children between them have arrived simultaneously and the owners of the house—two very excited grandparents, Emma and Timmy Hanbury—rush to the door to hug them all.

Marina, the eldest of the three siblings, and husband Ned Lambton and their four children, Stella, Claud, Acony, and Arthur, have driven from south-west London. Rose, number two in the pecking order, and wed to David Cholmondeley, with twin boys Oliver and Xan, and a daughter Iris, started off in Norfolk. The youngest, David Hanbury ("Uncle Dave"), has come for the weekend too.

The little ones, evidently familiar with the place, soon scramble to the kitchen to find their tea of egg and soldiers, laid out on Spode Malborough Sprays and Peter Rabbit china around a huge Moroccan vase filled with pheasant eye daffodils.

Below is a billiard room and fancy-dress trunk filled with Victorian clothes. Scattered about Timmy's study are leather backgammon and chess boards and when the sun appears a lovely battered croquet set is put out on the lawn. The TV sitting room terrace looks over a walled swimming pool with a barbeque recessed into the surrounding brick, and a twenty-minute walk from here through woodland, open fields, and long wispy grasses is a crescent-shaped beach below the clifftops.

From a child's point of view, you cannot help but feel that Wembury must be some kind of paradise. Rose remembers: "We were often picked up from school in Mum's little Citroën Deux Chevaux and driven down to the beach for barbeques and rock pool fishing."

But the pleasure is not just for the innocents. Emma and Timmy are known for being wonderful hosts, throwing wild and magical parties over the years, with colourful Raj tents dotted round the lawn serving as dance floors, dining areas, and lounge rooms and the house decorated with infamous humour and imagination. During an "Erotic, Exotic & Eccentric" party they laid palm leaves, pineapples, and sliced watermelons along the dining room table, while suspender belts were turned into curtain pelmets.

PAGE 219
Rose and her daughter Iris and Marina and her two daughters, Stella, left, and Acony, right, walk up the garden steps, past the discarded croquet set, from Wembury's south front. Marina wears crimson velvet Moroccan slippers.

PREVIOUS SPREAD
The sisters stand by the pool. Rose, left, wears a Moroccan ikat kaftan and Marina, right, is in an Indian cotton lily block-printed pool gown from the Villa Cetinale shop collection.

OPPOSITE
The downstairs loo at Wembury has Wellesley House prep school photographs of Marina and Rose's father, Timmy Hanbury, and their brother David Hanbury's certificate of a First Class degree in Engineering Science displayed among initialled coat brushes and a taxidermy sea turtle. The postcard on the table is of a 1918 Robert Morley painting of a terrier waiting for his master, sat in front of a World War I certificate of condolence announcing he has been killed and will not be returning. The framed notice it sits in is one written for Timmy's grandfather, Evan Hanbury, who was killed in World War I.

ABOVE
A painted wooden fish from Marina's childhood bedroom door.

PAGES 224–25
The kitchen at Wembury, with the family's impressive Spode Marlborough Sprays china collection displayed in the kitchen dresser.

PREVIOUS SPREAD
The Lily of the Valley guest bathroom with Santa Maria Novella Sapone al Melograno soap and Wiberg's Pine Bath Essence decanted into a glass bottle bathside.

ABOVE
The ceramic painted wreath hangs on the door of Rose's childhood bedroom.

OPPOSITE
Rose on the orangery steps in her antique silk kimono from the Hammersmith vintage fair.

FOLLOWING SPREAD
Rose and Marina as babies; childhood heights measured on the bathroom doorframe; a porcelain nodding-head Chinese figure; the dollhouse in front of Rose and Marina's butterfly wallpaper designed by their mother, Emma Hanbury; Rose's striped Afghani kaftan with Louboutin brogues and Lapima sunglasses; and family pictures displayed on the piano: all spotted at Wembury. The Rajasthani carved splash guards above the sinks can be found at Casa Marina in Italy, and the sample of Rose Cholmondeley Bramble wallpaper is based on a pattern found at Cholmondeley Castle.

One "Dangerous"-themed weekend yielded a chainsaw centrepiece, and a meteorite was heard whooshing across the lawn at midnight, product of the terrifying moonlit game of Fireball Hockey. It involves a flaming loo roll, doused in petrol and wrapped in chicken wire, used as a hockey ball—a game that was banned shortly after someone's hair caught fire.

But even on non-party days, every indoor or outdoor nook has something lovely, surprising, and beautiful to inspire or intrigue. Lining the hockey pitch—or lawn as they now refer to it—is an orangery with fragrant jasmine climbing the walls and red silk chandelier lampshades suspended from the glass ceiling. "We often had tea here as children and as teenagers arranged dinners lit by candlelight," Rose says.

Indoors, the plate and picture placement is particularly pleasing, as are the romantic wallpaper, Regency-style stencils, and lily of the valley bathroom tiles. There is a shell grotto in one bathroom, and embroidered Indian slippers for every size down to tiny baby's feet fanned out on a staircase corner stand. Indian wall hangings surrounding the basement stairwell, reminiscent of the steps down into the old Annabel's nightclub on Berkeley Square, give you the sensation of transitioning from one world to another. Rose explains: "When we were teenagers, Mum turned the basement into a night club for us, painting the whole place herself and hanging Moroccan lanterns and Suzanis from the walls. It felt a bit like an opium den." Emma confirms this was intentional.

As I get my little black book of interiors readied to note down the stencil specialist, tiler, and shellwork artist they employed, I learn it is all Emma's handwork, and the butterfly wallpaper is, in fact, hundreds of illustrated paper butterflies that she cut out and stuck on individually.

"She has a huge amount of energy, my mother," says Marina, who feels she has less of this creative ingenuity, which she thinks her sister Rose inherited, but certainly her mother's canny mindset about how to do interiors frugally. "I like to try and go to the source of things," she says. But where to start? While most of us would not know where to find beautiful chikankari embroidery, Italian marble, or ikat kaftans, the sisters seem undeterred by these investigative challenges. Accompanying their mother on trips to Delhi, Jaipur and Lucknow to source fabrics, tailors, and embroiderers for Marosa, the clothing company she ran for many years, must have played a part. She now sells interior items under the name Emma Hanbury.

As a teenager I often observed the sisters' shopping habits and was impressed by their wherewithal in finding the best flea markets or discount designer stores wherever they were in the world, be it Marrakesh, Goa, or Tuscany. In London, in the early 2000s, Marina introduced me to "Ken. Market" where racks of second-hand leather jackets and trousers could be found down a dark corridor off Kensington High Street. Steinberg & Tolkien on the King's Road was another favourite, stacked with white dresses from the Edwardian era up to the 1970s, and Rose was often among the first to sift through rails at the Hammersmith vintage fair's early morning opening or trawl the busy Friday stalls at Portobello.

A store called Voyage on the Fulham Road captured this boho spirit of marrying souk fabrics with London fashion. Marina visited it frequently but said she could never afford anything. "It was

PHILIP NAYLOR-LEYLAND

PORTRAIT OF A MAN

"YOU DON'T WANT dramatic all of the time," says the man whose style has not changed in thirty-five years. At 7.30am Sir Philip Naylor-Leyland wakes and goes out for a walk, with or without a dog, before a pot of tea for one and two crustless triangles of white toast with Rose's Lemon & Lime marmalade are consumed. He is at his desk by 9am. Lunch is at 1.15pm, dinner at 8.15pm (or 8.30pm when guests are staying). A stickler for punctuality, he is rarely late. One glance at his watch and an apology follows if he arrives somewhere at 5.39pm and he planned to be there at 5.38pm.

At sixty-eight, he cuts a tall, elegant figure and has an impressive crop of dark brown wavy hair with only a few grey whisps above the ears—a medical anomaly after six children. But perhaps planning diary dates two years in advance, organising minutiae onto spreadsheets, always knowing the weather forecast—partly for flying, partly for golf—and sticking to the same routines no matter what is going on around him, has kept him sane.

He runs three and half miles twice a week, which amounts to about 350 miles a year and roughly 7,000 in twenty, he has calculated. "I started getting fat in my late thirties and thought, this won't do ... It could potentially get rather expensive to have to buy new suits all the time."

Philip has two daytime outfits, replicated in quantity in his wardrobe, covering winter and summer with very slight variations based on who is in his company. His winter wear when in his office at Milton Hall, his home in the Cambridgeshire countryside, consists of a checked shirt, corn-coloured corduroys cut high on the waist, like all his trousers, a tweed jacket and a tie if he has meetings. During the summer he wears buff cotton trousers and a blue shirt with the sleeves rolled up and a tie if pertinent. A navy suit with braces is for London business; on winter evenings it is a black-tie dinner suit and on summer nights an ivory linen jacket replaces the black dinner jacket.

Every ten years, David Halliwell, who has been butler at Milton for twenty-three years, is asked to order five more checked shirts, five blue, three ivory, a dozen beige, and a dozen blue ribbed socks from the same establishments patronised a decade earlier. Recently, Viyella, a fabric company founded in 1784, changed its wool-to-cotton ratio in their shirting fabric, much to Philip's distress. Having asked the manufacturer to do a run of the old style just for him, he had to decline their minimum offer of fifty. "Madness! At the most I'll only get through twelve," he said. The grey morning suit in his cupboard is the same one he wore on his wedding day in 1980 and it has yet to be altered.

During a party to celebrate his fiftieth birthday, his son's twenty-first and the house's five hundredth anniversary, he wore his usual black-tie dinner suit and ivory shirt with patent leather mess wellingtons. After just four hours sleep, the next morning, following his 7.30am alarm, he dug out a pair of Levi's not worn since 1982. The shock to his family, nursing sore heads, was so extreme that they asked him to change into his "normal outfit" before they could stomach lunch.

At one stage it was rumoured trainers were not allowed in the dining room, and those who came to stay and knew about this peeve, would take great pleasure in watching an unsuspecting bohemian or

PAGE 238
Philip with his Jack Russell terrier, Paddy, at his elder daughter's wedding, photographed by Dafydd Jones.

OPPOSITE
Philip's octagonal bathroom with Cole & Son lilac wallpaper, freestanding bath, Badedas bath gelee, Floris Lily of the Valley, Rose Geranium, and Stephanotis bath essences, and Bohemian glass on the mantelpiece. Spot his wife, Isabella, caught in the reflection.

FOLLOWING SPREAD
The double flock wallpaper from Cole & Son called Committee Room Green—named after the committee room in the Palace of Westminster, designed by A.W.N. Pugin. Mr & Mrs George Fitzwilliam hang either side of the window where Philip dresses in his navy suit from Frank Hall in Market Harborough.

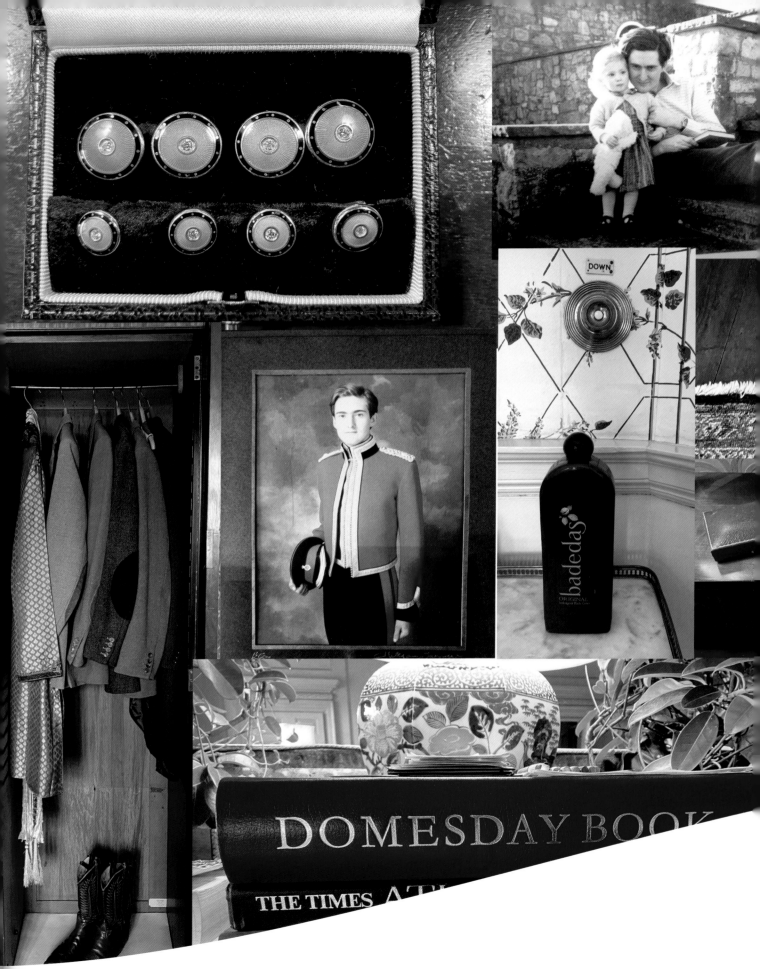

DOMESDAY BOOK

THE TIMES ATL

"

AFTER YOU HAVE CHILDREN, YOU HAVE
YOUR OWN WORLD. IT'S PROBABLY WHY I DON'T
GO TO THE THEATRE.

"

trendite enter the room in his dinner jacket and Converse, just to catch a glimpse of the subtle arched eyebrow that spoke a thousand words.

Despite the formalities and stories of him returning diners to their dressing rooms (exaggerated by his children to frighten visitors), Philip is in fact a generous host with a laissez-faire attitude to guests, and an ideal dinner partner as long as you appreciate good wit, like a healthy argument, do not take yourself too seriously and have a no-holds-barred attitude to subject matter. He is not one to talk about himself, though. He is more interested in other people and other things.

Musk mallow, herb robert, sandthorn, and greater knapweed are a handful of these. Obsessed with trees, wild flowers, and the natural habitat around him, he has incorporated a grass meadow into the garden with the purpose of nurturing as many of his favourite wild flowers as possible. Identifying, picking, and pressing hedgerow blooms with his young children was a favourite pastime and the season's first woodland violets often found their way into an egg cup on the breakfast table, for his eldest daughter.

He was brought up mainly between North Wales and London where his father, Vyvian, a landowner, and his mother, Elizabeth-Anne, an Egyptologist, lived, respectively. They had divorced when Philip was five, and so when he was not at boarding school he hopped between the two, as well as Milton, where his grandparents lived. Finishing his A-levels at Eton College at sixteen, he went on to Davies, Laing and Dick, a "crammer" in Holland Park, London, used to help sixth-form students enter Oxbridge.

Moving into his mother's house in Rutland Street put him a stone's throw from his newly discovered favourite shop, Deborah & Clare on Beauchamp Place. "It sold the most beautiful brightly coloured shirts with billowy sleeves and tight cuffs," he remembers.

So, with a trail motorbike to get to college, a freshly trimmed bouffant, crushed velvet bell-bottom trousers, and a rotation of Deborah & Clare shirts, 1960s London life began for Philip. His mother made the most of having her teenage son live with her, borrowing his shirts in his absence. They appealed to her "wacky" sense of colour. He explains: "Well, she had red hair, so she wore greens a lot, and garishly coloured silk patterned dresses. I thought she was very stylish."

Going on to describe pictures of her he admired from the 1950s when she wore sweaters with A-line skirts showing off her slender waist, he says: "Really, there is nothing better. When you see Grace Kelly or one of those women of that time in clothes like that, they look simply tremendous." At which point he checks himself "Why am I talking about clothes?!"

Not wanting to lose momentum I ask where his mother shopped. "She liked to buy cheaply, unlike my grandmother who was rumoured to have packed five suitcases and twelve hatboxes for Ascot and had a separate bank account for clothes so no one could see what she was spending." Some extraordinary items were found in her cupboards when she died, including a floor-length leopard-print rain mac.

Her daughter Elizabeth-Anne must have splashed out once though. "I know my mother had a Dior dress, because I was going to wear it one evening. Me and the lads were going to dress in drag and go out to a restaurant." As I express some surprise, he reacts casually: "Everyone was more camp in those days."

As neither Cambridge nor Oxford beckoned, he signed up for the army, moving to Dublin with his father in the interim, who paid for some flying lessons and at age seventeen Philip gained a Private Pilot Licence—something he has kept up. He describes the enjoyment: "It's an intellectual challenge involving different disciplines. It combines skill, which is rewarding, with a faint hint of danger."

Shortly after becoming a pilot, he went to work on the family farm in Wales. "There were big sheds full of cattle fed by a conveyor belt, which was always breaking down so one had to go and sort it out. There was a lot of slurry, I seem to remember. Anyway, it was quite jolly," he says.

In between shifts he ran up and down the hills to get into shape but in rather a "feeble way." "Had I known what I was going to encounter subsequently, I would've trained a bit harder. It was quite hardcore." His Brigade Squad at Pirbright performed ten-mile runs each day, carrying a twenty-pound pack and an assault rifle. Following this he would have to run up a sandbank with someone on his back. "I ended up with the PT instructor who was very large."

PREVIOUS SPREAD
Hawkes cufflinks sit serenely in a stud box. A kurta worn at an Indian wedding and Tony Lama cowboy boots bought in New York make incongruous wardrobe additions. Philip's favourite bath gelee is parked underneath the old Down bell, no longer in use. The two portraits are Philp with his elder daughter, and Philip, aged twenty-two, in his Life Guards mess uniform. The arched doorway designed by English architect Henry Flitcroft frames a view from the hall through to his study.

OPPOSITE
The other side of Philip's dressing room with his aunt Alathea Ward and the 10th Earl Fitzwilliam above the doors. The gentleman's press in fiddleback mahogany is the largest wardrobe in the house, albeit containing the fewest items.

FOLLOWING SPREAD
The family brushing room showing the uncovered sixteenth-century panelling and the original North Hall table on which Mrs George Fitzwilliam was laid out after she died to be viewed by the family and staff.

He describes sitting silently on his bed for hours, polishing his boots to present to the sergeant who would then throw them out of the window, and tell him to start again. He found that Sandhurst, though "not a walk in the park," paled in comparison, after which he was commissioned into the Life Guards, leaving at the end of his three-year Short Service Commission having attained the rank of Lieutenant.

Along with keeping to strict routines, organising others, and planning for unexpected eventualities—rather useful if you're planning on having half a dozen children—I wonder what else the army taught him, other than bad language. "Well, I can iron things. I don't, but I *could*. I can certainly polish boots. And I suppose it's left me with a conventional style I fall back on from time to time." Does a shirt with the sleeves rolled up to provide comfort from the heat and a tie worn in order not to appear disrespectful to others, ring a bell? He replies: "In the army, that was known as shirt sleeve order."

In 1976 he moved to New York with his new girlfriend, Isabella Lambton, to work in an investment bank and she as Andy Warhol's receptionist at the Factory, which had its perks. Evenings regularly ended at Studio 54, where Andy would whisk them past the queue of hopefuls and the doorman would bid them "evening," swiftly sliding open the rope. One weekend, when the artist was out of town, the couple took eager friends, who were visiting the city, to their regular haunt. Arriving at the door, Philip smiled familiarly at the doorman but was told "Back of the line, fella!"

Back to England, in 1980 Philip and Isabella married and two children followed closely. In 1987 his father died. Shortly after, aged thirty-seven, Philip was diagnosed with a malignant melanoma. Refusing to miss the cricket match for which his nine-year-old son had been chosen to keep wicket, he taped hospital devices to the inside of his tweed jacket and arrived pitch-side, with minutes to spare of course. In 1997, a decade after losing his father, his mother died at the same age of sixty-three. I ask if these things ever play on his mind? "Well, it played on my mind at sixty-three, briefly," he says, laughing. "Then I turned sixty-four. And it was fine." As I wonder if this inspired his exercise regime, he says: "I go exercising in order to drink and eat as much as I like."

Moving into Milton in 1999, renovations were made to prepare for the family's arrival. A lover of restoration and architectural detail, with a small pang of guilt he took out his mother's yellow paisley 1970s kitchen, restoring the sixteenth-century wood panelling underneath and making it the family's boot room. He points out with relish the grain on the floorboards showing the timbers were cut a certain way: "Quarter-sawn oak always looks very beautiful because you have these speckles in it called medullary rays."

Fanatical about detail, liking things done properly is something of a theme. Nicknamed Captain von Trapp for a stint when he insisted his children polished their shoes before school, as more offspring arrived, there was dissension in the ranks and standards slipped. Unable to insist on polished shoes for school *or* dinner, he simply asked that they wore *some* shoes, as opposed to none at all.

FOLLOWING SPREAD
*Philip walking Rufus
through the meandering
grass pathways in the
wildflower meadow he
designed, with Milton Hall
as the backdrop.*

OPPOSITE
*Philip's crocodile-skin cigar
case, softened with wear,
usually kept in his dinner
jacket pocket.*

Though the spreadsheets, itineraries, flight plans, weather reports, mealtime schedules, and boot polish are ever present, six children, six grandchildren and seven dogs later, he has mellowed and there is much more of the Swinging Sixties about him. Yet, he is still not one to let a detail slide. Nervously muttering the interviewee name and date into my recording equipment while reading my watch upside down, I notice him wind his Submariner and adjust his hearing aid. He then remarks: "I'm sorry to say it's not the eleventh of November. It's the fifteenth."

Standing corrected (I had almost forgotten who I was interviewing), I am amused and begin to relax.

For if you can find order and a sense of purpose in life and still take time to appreciate the beauty and detail of an inspiring but chaotic world, it can instil a sense of calm. In an era where few traditions are kept or standards held to esteem, there is something comforting about someone who bothers to keep them. But perhaps I have just grown used to him.

We share similarities, certainly many interests, but even so, sometimes I wish I was a bit more like my dad.

PAGES 254-55
A spreadsheet Philip keeps in his cupboard. The birdcage, with a photograph of Philip's mother behind, winds up with a large brass key and the taxidermy bird tweets when a little lever is pulled. A keen reader of P.G. Wodehouse, Philip has a collection of his works in Everyman's hardbacks, along with a well-thumbed pocket wildflower book in his study. Golden retriever Rufus sits in front of the fire with sister Ponder, who belongs to Philip's younger daughter. Rufus sleeps under the tennis rackets and dog leads at night. The little portrait in a china frame is Philip in Wales, aged eight, off to boarding school.

PAGES 256-57
Enjoying a Montecristo No. 3 in the Peterborough dining room at Milton, designed by Sir William Chambers in 1770. It is used as a sitting room to entertain guests after dinner. Philip wears his ivory summer dinner jacket and Tricker's of Jermyn Street velvet slippers.

PNL Packing List

Always	Outdoor	DJ	Shooting
Sponge Bag	Cap	Dinner Jacket	Plus Fours
Polishing Kit	Scarf	Evening Shirts	Shirt
Black Shoes	Barbour	Evening Socks	Vest
Brown Shoes	Boots	Bow Tie	Shooting Stockings
Shoe Trees	Gloves	Black Shoes	Garters
Stud Box			Long Johns
Collar Stiffeners			Jerseys
Clothes Brush			Shooting Gloves
Corduroys			Guns
Cotton Trousers			Cartridges
Socks			Cartridge Bag
Underpants			Earphones
Nightshirt			Barbour
Dressing Gown			
Shirts			
Ties			
Jersey			
Tweed Coat			
Suit			
Handkerchiefs			
Battery Charger			
Cigars			

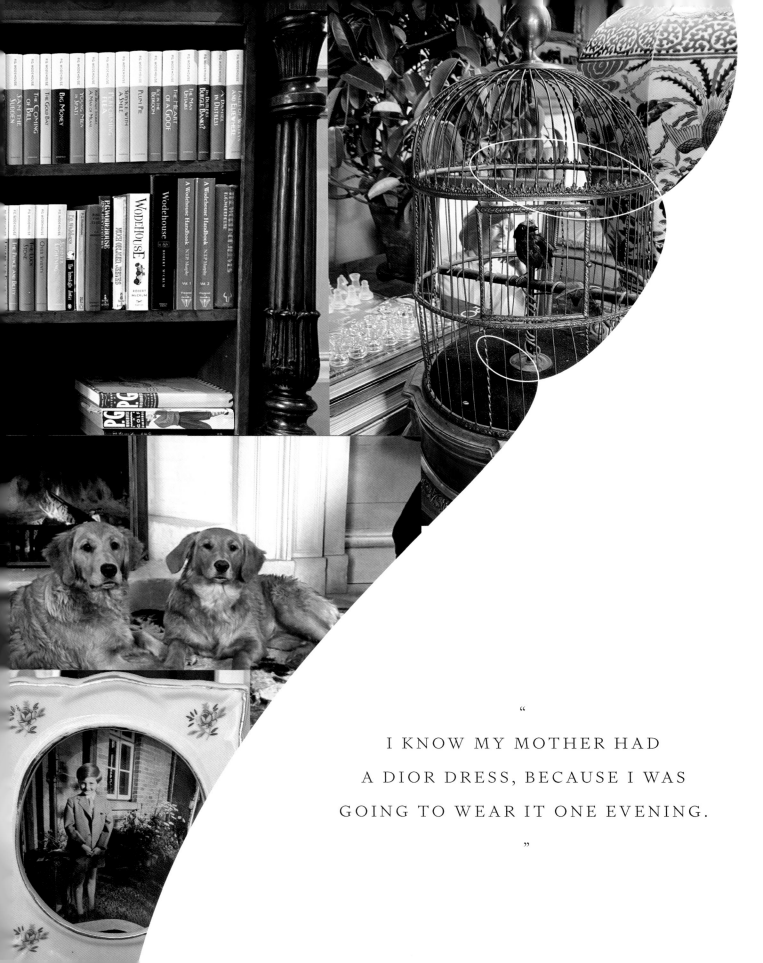

I KNOW MY MOTHER HAD
A DIOR DRESS, BECAUSE I WAS
GOING TO WEAR IT ONE EVENING.

...iaparelli

le 30 mai 2015

a very ambitious project—to be some sort of sun-fairy wonder-woman, but I got to work with the head of embroidery, and he helped me a lot." Fast-tracked to this department, she was able to conjure the magic she hoped for but with more freedom and intricacy than she had expected.

Sabine is witty, among other things, and also strikes me as someone very "particular." She makes careful choices with her words, which are always eloquent and thoughtful, so I am not surprised to hear she sent the first samples back. Maison Lesage revisited an embroidery technique that it had not used for decades, stuffing the sequinned pattern with cotton to produce *le relief* she felt sure the cape deserved. Three different types of gold sequins were picked out for the sun motif, to lessen the *moderne* feel. Two suns were also repeated on the front of the dress, their shining tendrils appearing to clasp her tiny waist; as well as on its sleeves, and on the ring cushion. Sabine's beautiful court shoes from Charlotte Olympia were covered in dress silk and sent to Lesage for gilding too.

Sabine designed earrings of fireballs, wore a gold necklace and diamond bracelet belonging to her mother—turning the latter into a hairpiece—and her hair was done with sweeping waves curling away from a chignon to signify the sun's rays. A magnificent piece of styling. A vision. A historic dress. And one little girl's dream complete.

But I wonder what started her fascination with high drama, cinema, and fashion. Sabine remembers being a "very observant, quiet child" always "fascinated by women" and the "allure" of someone with "style," on screen or in reality. She says very openly that she has always been influenced by everyone: "I'm a sponge. I've always looked up to women who are older, who have power, presence ... [and are] someone I'd like to be basically, which is a whole lot of other people than myself."

She talks of the "imprint" her Egyptian mother's sharp 1980s wardrobe left on her: the sleek and dramatic Yves Saint Laurent and Versace skirt suits. "I remember the shoulder pads and her long red nails," Sabine muses, as I note her own hands against her blue jeans and black sweater, elegantly painted a pillar-box red. Perhaps her admiration for Aunt Miraide, her Lebanese father's sister, who dressed like him in relaxed masculine shapes and tonal beige, sunk in too. "She wore a huge loose coat and those brown-colour glasses, that are neither sunglasses nor reading glasses but that very cool in-between shade. She had her hair back and would just be the coolest person in the room," she gushes.

And what of the sun? After her father left Lebanon in 1975 during the civil war and her mother left Egypt after her family's company was nationalised a few years later, their worlds collided in the still sunny but cooler and more peaceful Switzerland, where Sabine was born in 1984. Perhaps her heritage of sunny climates was enough to seep into her psyche, or maybe it came from the white light reflected off the snowy mountains surrounding the Geneva flat where she spent her first twelve years. Those glistening Mediterranean sunsets, sand, and blue-sky coloured mosques, and rust and yellow spiced powders from the markets in Beirut, where she spent her teenage years, must have played a part. It is clear in the way Sabine dresses and from the decoration in the couple's Mayfair flat, that light and bright colours are integral to

OPPOSITE
The spectacular grotto at Wormsley is an ode to Sabine's grandfather-in-law Paul Getty, who commissioned garden designers I & J Bannerman to build it shortly before he died.

ABOVE
A Schiaparelli embroidered ring cushion echoes the design of Sabine's wedding dress.

OPPOSITE
Sabine's satin Charlotte Olympia shoes were sent to Schiaparelli in Paris for embellishment.

BELOW
Spider-web embroidered Charlotte Olympia padded shoe trees with satin ribbons.

her very being. It is no coincidence then that she chose the light-emitting medium of jewellery with which to forge her career.

But I would still like to know, and ask a little tentatively, if she was in the end happy with her wedding outfit, and whether, given the chance, she would do it all over again. Her answer is that she feared the dress and cape belonged more in a fairy-tale wood or in a book such as this than in church, but above and beyond this she appreciates the inspiration behind it.

She says: "I think back and remember why I did it." In reference to the poignant moment in a woman's life when the girl takes one more step away from childhood and draws a line under it so as to make way for a new chapter, she says: "I honoured my inner child. In a way I was kind to her. I took the child and I took the dream along with me."

And in the names of her and Joe's children, Gene and Jupiter, the divine magic of dreams still twinkles and will be passed down inexorably.

The End

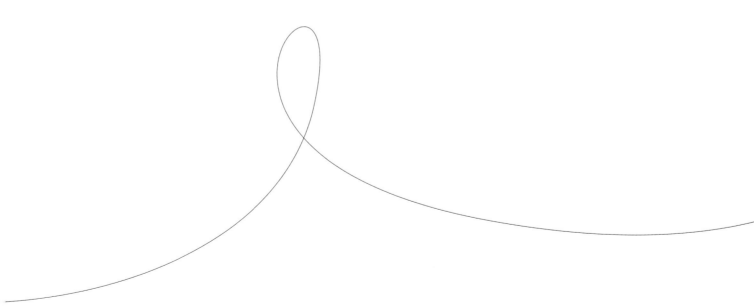

ACKNOWLEDGEMENTS

There have been so many kind and giving people out there happy to put me in touch with a friend, brother, godmother, agent, or hair stylist; provide a listening ear or gimlet eye, a welcome picture or a well-needed quote or detail; and play a vital role on one of our shoots: child or animal wrangling, art directing, assistant styling, reflector-holding, trouser-pressing, tea-brewing, or cocktail mixing.

I hope I've not forgotten anyone: Beatle and Jenny Lindsay-Fynn, Daisy Gilly from the London Film Academy, David Cholmondeley, David Halliwell, Dick Elcho, Duncan Campbell, Eleo Carson, Emma, Timmy, and Dave Hanbury, Guy Tobin from the Rose Uniacke interiors team, Hannah Warner, Jamaica Radcliffe, James Peill, James Reginato, Jane Ormsby Gore, Janet Slee, John Finlay, John Ingledew, Kelly Robinson, Laura Cavendish, Michael Davis, Melanie de Blank, Molly Miller Mundy, Ned Durham, Nicholas Cookson, Nina Ferguson, Nina Flohr, Pearl van den Ende, Prue Leith, Rifat Ozbek, Sophia Pilkington, Sylvie Mullens, Tom Felton, Victoria Stapleton, Vin + Omi, Virginia Bonham Carter, and William Naylor-Leyland.

Thank you to those who have appeared in my book: Victoria Grant, Luke Edward Hall, Lulu Guinness, Beata Heuman, Zandra Rhodes, Lyndell Mansfield, Nicky Haslam, Susie Lau, Charlie Casely-Hayford, Alice Temperley, Philip Colbert, Martha Sitwell, Andrew Logan, Marina Durham, Rose Cholmondeley, Philip Naylor-Leyland, and Sabine Getty. It was with an open-minded and open-hearted attitude that they did and the book is all the more wonderful for it.

I wanted to acknowledge the true force of nature that was Lyndell Mansfield, who sadly died on October 1, 2021, before this book was published. Lyndell was untouchably unique, a true one-off, a lone star, an extraordinary talent, and everything this book stands for. I was deeply saddened by her passing, not least because I felt I had met a kindred spirit and someone whose friendship I hoped would become a long one. I hope she and her loved ones feel I told her story in the spirit of Lyndell and that her chapter does justice to her memory.

There were some particularly special children who sat beautifully for photographs and were exceedingly helpful while shooting: Alma Finlay, Fox Temperley von Bennigsen Mackiewicz, Ollie, Xan, and Iris Cholmondeley, and Stella, Claud, and Acony Lambton.

Animals: three alpacas and various chickens (whose names escape me), dogs Guinness, Ethel, Trevor, Merlin, Rufus, and Vera, and Florence the Flemish rabbit.

Thank you to spectacular florists wildatheart.com and thecountrygardenflorist.co.uk, Perrier-Jouët champagne and Café Royal for your generosity.

A very special thanks to the extraordinary make-up artists Charlotte Cowen, Martha Sitwell, and Tania Grier, hair stylists Jenny Green, Natalia Souza, and Snowden Hill who lent their time and expertise to our beautiful photoshoots.

Additional heartfelt thanks to our first photography assistant Kwesi Mcleod, second photography assistants Noah Sagum and Eleanor Jenkins, videographer Justice Akushie Junior (from the London Film Academy), and film editor Geordie Leyland.

And finally, on our shoot team, but by no means least, Andrew Farrar, who provided the book's most spectacular images. His brilliant eye—particularly for portraiture and expert editing—shines on the pages of this book.

Thank you to the Rizzoli team who guided me along this journey, in particular my publisher, Charles Miers, and my completely delightful, diplomatic, funny, and deeply conscientious editor, Giulia Di Filippo, whose listening ears I fear may have dropped off by now.

Thank you to the design team Charlotte Heal and Kat Jenkins, whose initial ideas for the book design continued to inspire us throughout the process.

A BIG thank-you to my mum and dad, Isabella and Philip, brothers Geordie and Edley, and sister Beatrix, sisters-in-law Florence and Vinnie, and brother-in-law Bug Hedley, friends Anna Mathias, Amber Guinness, and Matthew Bell—and to all those who listened to my chapters and my woes and gave well-needed feedback.

Most of all thank you to my husband, Charlie Day, who has been my support throughout this process, listened to most chapters, painted a Do Not Disturb sign for my office door (which he often ignored), put the kids to bed many more than his fair share of times to help me meet deadlines, and told me things I did not want to hear when I asked for his input. A hugely talented creative force in his own right, his views mean a lot to me. His support has been invaluable.

And almost final apologies to my children, Aubrey and Fleetwood. The one redeeming moment of time away from you, that felt worth it, was when you both (aged five and one) tottered into my barn office one afternoon, which was covered wall-to-wall in book images, writing, and collages. You looked up at my walls, uncommonly silent. "The lady with the rabbit's my favourite," the five-year-old announced suddenly. "Look—a big egg!" said the one-year-old. Then the older one said, "Wow Mummy, what is this?" I told him it was my book I'd been working very hard on for three years, to which he replied: "Why did you make it so long?" It was a labour of love. But fair point. I hope you can be proud of me one day.

Lastly, thank you to Quies wax earplugs. Without you there would be no book.

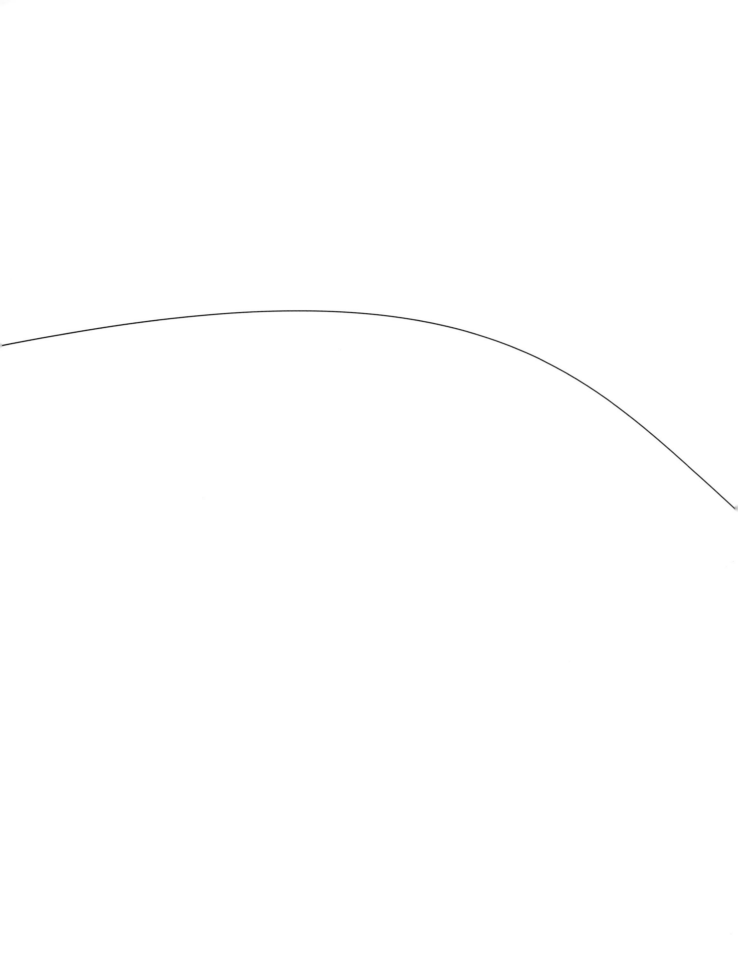

First published in the United States of America in 2022 by
Rizzoli International Publications, Inc.
300 Park Avenue South
New York, NY 10010
www.rizzoliusa.com

Publication © 2022 Rizzoli International Publications, Inc.
Text © 2022 Violet Naylor-Leyland
Photography © 2022 Andrew Farrar

Publisher: Charles Miers
Senior editor: Giulia Di Filippo
Text editors: Linda Schofield and Victoria Brown
Production manager: Maria Pia Gramaglia

Designed by Charlotte Heal Design

Printed in Singapore

2022 2023 2024 2025 2026 / 10 9 8 7 6 5 4 3 2 1

ISBN: 978-0-8478-7218-3

Library of Congress Control Number: 2022935445

Visit us online:
Facebook.com/RizzoliNewYork
Twitter: @Rizzoli_Books
Instagram.com/RizzoliBooks
Pinterest.com/RizzoliBooks
Youtube.com/user/RizzoliNY
Issuu.com/Rizzoli

Jacket photography: © Andrew Farrar

Additional Photography Credits
pp. 67, 70–71, 72: Copyright © Simon Brown; p. 92: Copyright © Bridie O'Sullivan;
p. 178, bottom left: Copyright © Marcus Dawes; p. 211, bottom right: Copyright © Si Morgan;
p. 238: Copyright © Dafydd Jones